English for academic study:

Listening

Course Book

Colin Campbell
and Jonathan Smith

University of Reading

Credits

Acknowledgements

Published by
Garnet Publishing Ltd.
8 Southern Court
South Street
Reading RG1 4QS, UK

Copyright © 2007 University of Reading's Centre for Applied Language Studies, The University of Reading, and the authors.

The right of Colin Campbell and Jonathan Smith to be identified as the authors of this work has been asserted by them in accordance with the Copyright, Designs and Patents Act 1988.

ISBN: 978 1 85964 986 6

British Library Cataloguing-in-Publication Data
A catalogue record for this book is available from the British Library.

Production
Project manager: Maggie MacIntyre
Editorial team: Emily Clarke, Richard Peacock, Rod Webb
Art director: Mike Hinks
Design and layout: Nick Asher
Illustration: Doug Nash
Audio: Matinée Sound and Vision
Video: Tom, Dick and Debbie Productions

Every effort has been made to trace copyright holders and we apologise in advance for any unintentional omissions. We will be happy to insert the appropriate acknowledgements in any subsequent editions.

Printed and bound
Printed in Malta through Printworks Int. Ltd.

A large number of people contributed in different ways to the production of this book, although all responsibility for any mistakes remains ours alone.

We would like to thank the following for their permission to use extracts from the lectures that were originally recorded as part of the British Academic Spoken English (BASE) corpus:

Professor Michael Utton, Professor Alan Roberts (Rennes Business School, France), Dr Steve Wiggins, Alan Rowley, Dr Clare Furneaux, Dr Elizabeth Gaffan, Dr Colin Beardsley, Professor Peter Roach and Dr Rupert Loader.

In addition we would like to thank Shelagh Tonkyn for permission to use an extract from a lecture on Magistrates' Courts given at the University of Reading, and acknowledge the influence of Tony Lynch's ideas on note-taking in Unit 4 of this book.

Our colleagues, Dr Paul Thompson and Sarah Creer, were very helpful in making the BASE corpus available and accessible to us, and in suggesting suitable lectures from the corpus.

The following colleagues gave invaluable feedback on parts of this book, and their contribution is gratefully acknowledged: Emma Grenside, Bruce Howell, Anne Pallant, John Slaght, Lucy Watson and Sebastian Watkins. We would also like to thank Nicola Taylor and her in-sessional students for giving us the opportunity to trial some of the material in the book.

Contents

Introduction

Aims of this book:

This book has been designed with two main aims in mind:

- to help you better understand spoken English, particularly the spoken English of academic lectures.
- to help you develop your note-taking skills while listening.

Video/audio recordings

Many of the lecture extracts in this book are based on transcripts of authentic lectures given at the University of Reading. These lectures were given to audiences of British and international students as part of their normal degree programmes. Although the extracts have been re-recorded to ensure clarity, the language and content of these lectures have been maintained, to ensure that you are provided with listening practice that closely simulates listening to and note-taking from real academic lectures.

The lecture extracts are taken from a range of academic fields, including investment banking, development economics, marketing, psychology and linguistics. Although the original lectures were intended for students doing degrees in these subjects, we have chosen extracts that should be accessible to a general audience of students.

Other extracts have been written specially for this book, but have also been designed to reflect features of authentic academic lectures.

Structure of the book

Apart from the first unit, all the units are divided into two sections; macro-skills and micro-skills.

Macro-skills include such things as:

- making use of lecture introductions;
- note-taking;
- recognising the structure of lectures.

Micro-skills focus on linguistic features of spoken English such as:

- recognising words that are spoken quickly and are not stressed;
- recognising where one spoken word ends and the next begins;
- word stress and sentence stress.

In these units you will also find items called *Sound advice*, which either summarise key points from the unit or present advice on listening strategies.

At the end of the book you will find transcripts for all the texts in the book. Your teacher will draw your attention to these transcripts and will, occasionally, after you have completed the main listening tasks, give you the opportunity to listen to the recording and follow the transcript at the same time. Doing this will help you learn the spoken forms of words that you may only know in their written form.

Vocabulary

Although the recordings in the book may not be related to your particular subject, you will find a lot of useful vocabulary in this book.

There are different types of vocabulary that you may find useful:

- academic words – these are words that occur frequently in many different academic subjects, so whatever your degree subject, it is important to learn how to use these words.

- non-technical topic words – many of the recordings use sets of topic vocabulary which will be useful to students on almost all degree courses; for example, the text on market research contains many words connected with surveys and questionnaires and statistics.

- subject-specific words – some of the recordings contain words which will be of particular interest to students of specific subjects. For example, there is an extract on social learning which will be of particular interest to students planning to study psychology.

Listening outside the classroom

Your listening will improve more quickly if you practise outside the classroom. You can do this in a variety of ways, for example, talking with friends, listening to the radio or watching TV, or working with independent study materials.

You will find *Sound advice* sections in most units in this book, and these contain useful advice for improving your listening, but here are some more ideas.

- There are a number of good websites which provide practice in listening to academic lectures. If you go to the EAS website (enter through http://www.englishforacademicstudy.com) you will find links to these sites.

- A wide range of vocabulary is part of the key to success in listening. You should keep a record of new words or phrases that you meet, and you should make sure you note down the pronunciation, particularly if it does not fit in with pronunciation patterns you are familiar with. Ask the teacher to model the pronunciation if you are not sure of it.

- There are several dictionaries on CD-ROM, which link with *Word* documents and web pages, so that you can hear the pronunciation (and see the meaning) of a word on screen, either by moving the mouse pointer over a word or by clicking on it. The *Macmillan English Dictionary* and *Longman Dictionary of Contemporary English* both have good CD-ROM versions. Think about buying one, because it will be useful, not just on this course, but in your later studies.

1 Listening and lectures

In this unit you will:
- discuss the different situations in which you have to listen;
- identify what factors influence your ability to understand;
- learn about features of lectures in different academic cultures.

Task 1: Listening in different languages

In pairs or small groups, discuss your answers to these questions.

a) In your own language, which of these types of listening do you think is more difficult or requires more attention? Why?

- listening to a friend as part of your conversation with them;
- listening to the radio;
- listening to announcements at a crowded railway station;
- listening to an academic lecture.

b) What experiences have you had of listening to English?

c) What type of listening in English do you find more demanding/less demanding?

Task 2: Issues in understanding spoken English

2.1 What makes it difficult to listen to and understand spoken English? Here are some factors which affect comprehension.

- the speed at which someone is speaking;
- background noise;
- _____ ;
- _____ ;
- _____ .

With your partner, add two or three more factors to this list.

2.2 1.1 Listen to part one of a talk in which a teacher describes some of the problems of listening.

a) Which of the factors in the list in Task 2.1 did she talk about?

b) Which other factors did she talk about?

c) After talking about the factors which affect listening, she goes on to discuss two additional problems that students may have. What are they?

2.3 🔊 **1.2** Now listen to part two of the talk, in which the teacher illustrates the two problems she has introduced. The teacher asks you to write down a phrase. Do this as you listen.

Does this example make the points clearer?

2.4 🔊 **1.3** Listen to part three of the talk and complete this excerpt by writing between two and six words in each space.

> So what is the solution to these two problems? Well, firstly you need to get as much practice listening to natural speech as possible. Listen to
> _____ and try to develop your
> understanding of how words and phrases are really pronounced, not how you _____ pronounced. Secondly, you _____ that when you listen you may misunderstand what is said. So you need to be ready to_____ _____ about your understanding of the meaning, if what you hear _____
> compared to what you understood before. And this means taking a flexible, open-minded approach to listening.

2.5 Reflect on the talk you just listened to.

a) Did you have any difficulties doing this activity?

b) If so, why do you think you had problems?

c) Were they the same problems the lecturer talked about?

Task 3: Listening to lectures

You are going to a listen to a teacher talking about the differences he perceives between lectures in the UK and in China.

3.1 Before you listen, talk to a partner about your experiences of lectures in your own country and/or in the country where you are studying. Think about:

● what the lecturers did, e.g., *read from notes, used visuals, asked questions,* etc.;

● what the students did, e.g., *asked questions, took notes,* etc.

3.2   Note-taking.

In the first part of the talk, the teacher describes:

- what his main interest is;
- where he got his information about lectures in China;
- the survey he did and the students he talked to.

○ **1.4** Listen to part one of the talk and make some brief notes about these three points.

3.3   Compare what you have written with other students.

a)   Did you record the same information?

b)   Could you have recorded the information in different ways using fewer words/different words? How?

3.4   ○ **1.5** In part two of the talk, the speaker first talks about some of the characteristics of lectures in China and then compares these with lectures in the UK. Listen and make brief notes on the main points he makes.

China	UK

3.5   Compare your notes with other students.

a)   Did you record the same information?

b)   Could you have recorded the information in different ways, using fewer words/different words? How?

3.6   Responding to the talk.

Work in groups. Discuss your reactions to what the speaker said.

a)   If you are from China, do you agree with what the speaker reported about lectures in China?

b)   If you are from another country, are the lectures in your country more like the British system, the Chinese one, or a combination of both?

c)   Have you already listened to lectures in English?

d)   Did you take notes (in English or your own language) during the lectures you have attended?

e)   Was it difficult to take notes? If so, why?

f)   What did you do before and after your lectures to help you understand more fully and remember the content?

Summary of the main points studied in this unit

- Understanding the factors which affect your ability to listen to and understand spoken English.

- Considering differences between lectures in your country and in the UK.

- Recognising main points while listening.

2 Introductions to lectures

In this unit you will:
- look at how a lecture introduction can help you to understand the lecture better;
- practise making notes on introductions to lectures;
- learn how to recognise words that may be pronounced differently to the way you expect them to be.

Task 1: Thinking about introductions

1.1 What do you expect the lecturer to talk about in the introduction to a lecture?

1.2 Think of lectures you have heard. Did the lecturers try to make the structure of the lecture obvious to students? If so, how?

1.3 Two students took notes on the introduction to a lecture about migration. Look at the notes they took. How are the notes different?

Student 1:

> Migration from new EU countries, e.g., Poland - effect on UK econ., etc.

Student 2:

> Not EU migration BUT internal UK migration, e.g., country ⟶ city

1.4 ◗ 2.1 Listen to the introduction. Which student understood what the lecturer was going to talk about? Why do you think the other student made a mistake? Which words in the introduction signal what the lecturer will talk about?

> **Sound advice:** In an introduction, the speaker may define the scope of the lecture, but he may do this by explaining what will not be discussed, as well as what will be discussed.

Task 2: Functions and language of lecture introductions

The items in the left-hand column of the table on the next page show what lecturers commonly do in introductions.

a) Tick those items you discussed in Tasks 1.1 and 1.2 and make sure you understand what is meant by the other items.

b) Match each item with a statement from the right-hand column. All the statements are taken from introductions to lectures.

What lecturers do	Lecturer statements
a) limit the scope of the lecture; in other words, say what they will talk about and what they will not talk about	**i)** There are in a sense two themes – there's a qualitative stream of market research and there's a quantitative stream. I'm going to deal with basically the quantitative stream of data collection first.
b) comment on a theory they have just described	**ii)** However, that's not the type of migration I want to look at today. What I want to look at is internal migration, i.e., the movement of people from country to city, and vice versa, and from one city to another.
c) preview the content or structure of the current lecture	**iii)** Sara Shettleworth has a superb chapter on social learning, and I'm going to mention just a few of the examples that she mentions.
d) refer to research in the subject – this often includes mentioning specific reading material	**iv)** What I want to do first is just to, because I know some of you are not from the EU, is just give a very simple introduction to European Union institutions.
e) give background information to the lecture topic	**v)** I undertook a study in the middle eighties and it was quite easy for me to find 22 markets.
f) introduce different approaches to the subject	**vi)** I'll be giving you a handout with these quotes, so you don't have to write them down verbatim.
g) refer to what students should/should not write down	**vii)** My critique about the theory of perfect contestability is that if you change the assumptions slightly, the predictions change dramatically. It's very unstable.
h) indicate that they are referring back to previous lectures and remind students of the content of those lectures	**viii)** Last term we looked at how accounting systems were different. We looked at France and Germany and the Netherlands, and so forth, to see how the financial reports are different.
i) explain the lecturer's own interest in the subject, for example, any research they have done	**ix)** So today's session – I'm going to talk about the local environment, the role of local government, and also look at the interaction with the community.

Task 3: Listening to lecture introductions

You are going to listen to the introductions to three different lectures. Before you listen to each introduction you will do some activities to help you anticipate the content of the lectures.

3.1 The first lecture is entitled *Britain and European Monetary Union*. Before you listen, discuss these questions with another student.

a) What is the EMU?

b) Is Britain a member of the EMU?

c) What do you think is Britain's attitude to the EU? And to the USA?

Before you listen, check that you understand these phrases from the lecture.

> **single currency   opt out   the Commonwealth   Eurozone**

3.2 2.2 Listen to the introduction to the lecture about Britain and the EMU and identify which aspects from the check list in Task 2 the lecturer appears to be using.

3.3 The second lecture is entitled *Globalisation*. Before you listen, discuss these questions with another student.

a) What does 'globalisation' mean to you?

b) What kind of people does it affect?

c) Which department of the university do you think the lecturer is from?

Before you listen, check that you understand these words and phrases from the lecture.

> **stockbrokers   global tycoons   media empires   sociologist   implications**

3.4 2.3 Listen to the introduction to the lecture about globalisation and identify which aspects from the check list the lecturer appears to be using.

3.5 The third lecture is entitled *Magistrate's Courts*. Before you listen, discuss these questions with another student.

a) How many different types of courts do you have in your country?

b) What problems do the different courts deal with?

Before you listen, check that you understand these phrases from the lecture.

> **non-criminal matters   maintenance of children   criminal offences**

3.6 ◯ **2.4** Listen to the introduction to the lecture about magistrate's courts and identify which aspects from the check list the lecturer appears to be using.

Note: At the beginning of the lecture the speaker refers to 'John', the person who has introduced her.

Task 4: Micro-skills: Word stress

One problem faced by many international students is that they may not recognise the spoken forms of words which they might easily understand when reading. This is partly because words are sometimes not pronounced in the way students expect them to be.

4.1 ◯ **2.5** Listen and complete this sentence taken from the introduction to *Britain and European Monetary Union*, which you have already listened to.

> However, _____, I am going
> to spend most of the time today talking about why Britain _____
> _____ the euro, and then about whether I think that Britain
> might join the Eurozone in the future and in what circumstances.

a) Were the missing words ones you already knew?

b) If so, and you did not recognise them, why didn't you recognise them?

4.2 ◯ **2.6** Listen to these two sentences from the lecture on magistrate's courts. Write one word in each space.

> So, for example, in the case of family break-up, it would involve making
> parental _____ orders where the parents can't agree on how much
> _____ time each parent should have with the child.
>
> What we are mainly _____ with today is the criminal court,
> and that is what I am going to spend most of my time talking about
> this morning.

a) How do you pronounce the words you have written?

b) The first syllable of each word is spelt the same, but in the second extract it is pronounced differently. Why?

4.3 Put the words in the box into the correct column according to their word stress pattern.

> access   account   adapt   aspect   assist   assume
>
> connect   consist   consume   contact   context   control
>
> process   produce (v)   product   promise   protect   provide

Oo	oO

How do you know if the stress in two-syllable words falls on the first syllable or the second?

4.4 🔘 2.7 Listen to this recording about security and computers and complete the text, writing one word in each space. The words you need are from Task 4.3.

> Security is an important _____ of using a computer that many people do not pay much attention to. If you buy a laptop or personal computer, you will probably want to _____ to the Internet. If so, it is important that you install security software which will protect it from attack by viruses or spyware. There is a wide range of _____ available on the market, which are relatively cheap and which _____ a variety of different features. For example, in addition to checking their computer for viruses, parents can use the software to _____ which websites their children can _____. You should not _____, however, that you are 100 per cent safe if you are using such security software. You should make sure that you have backup copies of your work, and you should be very careful about keeping important information, such as bank _____ details, on your computer.

4.5 ◐ 2.8 Listen to this recording about competition between large supermarket chains and small, local shops and complete the text by writing one word in each space. This time the words are not from Task 4.3, but they all begin with con~, pro~ or a~.

> Because of planning restrictions, the large UK supermarket chains are looking to expand their businesses and increase _____, by opening smaller "convenience stores". Organisations representing small, independent shops _____ that they now face unfair competition from the large chains. And they _____ the large chains of a number of practices that make it difficult for them to compete. Firstly it is _____ that below-cost pricing is used by large supermarkets to force smaller, local shops out of business. Secondly, the large chains often buy up land which is not immediately used, and this prevents smaller local businesses from entering the market.
>
> There is also some _____ that the large chains are treating their suppliers unfairly. Farmers claim that they are being paid less for their products, and are reluctant to complain for fear of losing key _____. However, supermarkets argue that the _____ is the best regulator of the market.

Now look at the words you have written into the spaces. Does the stress fall on the first or second syllable? How do you pronounce these words?

4.6 Put the words in the box into the correct column according to their word stress pattern.

> decent   decide   decline   defend   delay   dentist
>
> effect   emerge   equal   even   event   expert   extinct
>
> reckon   reflect   rely   report   reptile   rescue

Oo	oO

4.7 ◐ 2.9 Listen to this recording about the effect of global warming on numbers of polar bears and complete the text by writing one word in each space. The words you need are from Task 4.6.

Wildlife _____ predict that numbers of polar bears will _____ by at least 50 per cent over the next 50 years because of global warming. Polar bears _____ on sea ice to catch seals for food, and it has _____ that ice floes in the Arctic are disappearing at an alarming rate. Scientists _____ that the animals are already beginning to suffer the _____ of climate change in some parts of Canada, and if there is any further _____ in tackling this problem, polar bears may be _____ by the end of the century.

4.8 ◗ **2.10** Listen to this recording about monitoring water levels in rivers and complete the text by writing one word in each space. This time the words are not from Task 4.6, but they all begin with *de~*, *re~*, or *e~*.

Scientists are now able to monitor river levels using information from satellites by using a computer programme _____ by researchers at De Montfort University in Leicester. Satellites have been able to measure the height of the sea by timing how long it takes to _____ a beam bounced back off waves. But until now interference from objects on the banks of rivers has made it impossible to measure river levels.

However, the new programme, which is based on data collected over the last _____ , is specially _____ to filter out this interference. This new technology will be particularly useful in monitoring river levels in _____ areas. It will, for example, enable scientists to _____ river level patterns over the _____ Amazon river basin, contributing towards our understandings of climate change.

Now look at the words you have written into the spaces. Does the stress fall on the first or second syllable? How do you pronounce these words?

Summary of main points studied in this unit

- Identifying what a lecturer is doing in the introduction of a lecture.
- Practising understanding introductions of lectures.
- Understanding word stress and the effect this has on the pronunciation of weak syllables.

Identifying key ideas in lectures

In this unit you will:
- practise identifying the key points a lecturer wants to make;
- distinguish key points from examples;
- use your understanding of examples to deduce key points;
- develop your understanding of relationships between ideas;
- learn patterns of pronunciation and word stress in word families.

Task 1: Thinking about key ideas

In pairs or small groups, discuss these questions.

a) Why is it important to recognise key ideas (or main points) in a lecture?

b) Why do lecturers use examples?

Task 2: Lecture on franchising: Part one

2.1 You are going to listen to the first part of a lecture on franchising. Before you listen, discuss the following questions in pairs.

a) What is franchising?

b) Can you think of any businesses that are run as franchises?

2.2 **3.1** Listen to part one of the lecture. This part can be divided into three clear sections. From the list here, identify the three sections and put them in the correct order.

a) _____ a definition of franchising

b) _____ examples of successful franchises

c) _____ one reason for setting up a franchise business

d) _____ how franchising works

e) _____ the types of business that are suitable for franchising

2.3 **3.2** Listen to the first section again.

a) Why does the lecturer talk about hairdressing salons?

b) Here are some points he makes in this section. Which do you think is the key idea in this section? What is the relationship between the key idea and the other points?

i) You may need large amounts of money or to bring in new skills to expand your business.

ii) As a business expands, the owner will not have the same amount of personal control over the operation of the business as he used to.

iii) As successful businesses develop, they often reach a stage when expansion brings risks.

iv) You can minimise the risks of developing your business by franchising it.

2.4 🌓 **3.3** In the second section, the lecturer gives a definition of franchising. Here are a few terms that he introduces. After you have heard this section again, discuss with your partner what they mean in the context of the lecture.

> **franchisor   franchisee   trademark   trade name   package**
>
> **untrained person   continual assistance**

2.5 🌓 **3.4** Listen to the third section again.

a) What does the franchisor provide to the franchisee?

b) What does the franchisee give in return?

Task 3: Lecture on franchising: Part two

3.1 The lecturer begins this part by saying, "There are a number of issues that you need to consider when deciding whether or not to franchise your business."

What do you think he will talk about next?

3.2 🌓 **3.5** Listen to part two of the lecture. The lecturer makes three or four main points. Note down what these main points are. You need to write down five to 15 words for each point.

Compare your notes with another student. Have you identified the same main points?

3.3 The lecturer uses signposting language to indicate that he is going to make key points. For example, for the first point, he says:

"Firstly, there needs to be ..."

Now look at the transcript for this part of the lecture on pages 59 and 60 and find other examples of signposting language.

3.4 🌓 **3.6** Listen to the first section of part two again.

a) To support his main point, the lecturer gives two reasons and two examples. What are they?

b) Do they help make his point clearer? If so, how?

3.5 🌓 **3.7** Listen to the second section of part two again.

a) What point does he make about buying supplies in bulk?

b) How is this point related to the main point in this section?

c) Now look at the following excerpt. Having made the main point, the speaker repeats the idea twice. Underline the words in the excerpt where he repeats the idea.

In addition – and this is fairly obvious – you will need a fairly wide margin between cost and income. Remember that the gross margin needs to provide a return on the investment to both the franchisor and the franchisee. So you will need to keep costs low and prices as high as the market will bear. One advantage of a franchise operation is that supplies can be bought in bulk across the whole franchise, which will help to keep costs down. But you can see that franchising would be unsuitable in a market where the margin between cost and income is very narrow.

3.6 ○ **3.8** Listen to the third section of part two again. In this part, the lecturer talks about:

- training and support;
- the operating manual;
- developing skills quickly.

a) How are these three ideas related to one another?

b) What point does he make about previous experience?

Task 4: Lecture on franchising: Part three

4.1 ○ **3.9** In part three, the lecturer continues to discuss some of the issues that need to be considered when trying to decide whether or not to franchise your business.

a) Listen and note down the main points the lecturer makes.

b) Compare your notes with another student. Have you identified the same main points?

4.2 ○ **3.10** Another technique used by the lecturer to highlight ideas is to stress key words or phrases. Listen to the first section of part three again and complete the excerpt by writing one to three words in each space. It should be relatively easy to do this, because all the missing words or phrases are stressed by the speaker.

One further issue you may need to consider is whether the business is _____ to other geographical areas. If you have developed your business serving one particular part of the country and you want to set up a franchise network covering a _____, the whole country for example, another thing you will have to consider is whether there is a _____ for your product or service in different regions. It may be, for example, that competition in other parts of the country may be so _____ that it is difficult for franchisees to _____, or that for localised _____ or _____ reasons the business may not be as profitable.

Notice that again the lecturer uses signposting language to indicate he is beginning a new point.

4.3 **3.11/3.12** In the last two sections of part three, the lecturer explains the importance of protecting the brand. Listen and note down the different ways in which this can be done.

4.4 Now look at the following excerpt.

a) Underline the signposting language used to highlight key points.

b) **3.11/3.12** Now listen and circle any key words or phrases the lecturer stresses.

> Finally, when you are setting up a franchise network, you will need to bear in mind that you will be losing direct control of the way your brand is perceived by the customer, so this brings me to my last point, which is to emphasise the importance of protecting your brand. I am sure you are all aware that it often takes a long time to establish a distinctive brand with a valuable reputation, but that this reputation can be damaged comparatively quickly if, for example, quality standards are not consistently applied. The detailed operating manual that I referred to earlier will play a role in maintaining the brand but, just as important, you need to take care selecting franchisees and monitoring their operations. In addition to checking that franchisees have the relevant skills and experience to run a successful business, you also need to ensure that they share the same business values as you, that they accept the importance of maintaining the brand and that they are clear about what they can or can't change about the way the business is run – so people who are very individualistic will probably not make good franchisees.
>
> The written agreement between the franchisor and the franchisee should specify very clearly what performance and quality standards are expected, and much of the initial training will be ensuring that staff have the skills to achieve these standards. However, regular visits to franchise units are essential in ensuring that the standards are being applied consistently and uniformly, and ongoing training may be necessary to deal with issues that are uncovered in these visits. Protecting the brand is ultimately in the interests of both the franchisor and the franchisee, because for the franchisee one of the main advantages of running a franchise is that they are buying into and helping to consolidate an established brand.

You may also notice that the speaker sometimes pauses after key points.

Sound advice

- As you listen, try to keep in mind the key ideas and relate any new information you hear to those ideas.
- Listen for signposting language, stressed words or phrases and pauses, as indicators of key points.
- If you do not understand a key point, listen for any examples which may help you to recover the meaning.

Task 5: Micro-skills: Word families (1)

You can extend your vocabulary by learning groups of words which have the same basic form and which are often related in meaning.

Examples:

Noun	Verb	Adjective
pr<u>o</u>duct, production, productivity	pro<u>du</u>ce	productive
definition	define	definite, definitive
economy, economics, economist	economise	economic, economical

5.1 Practice the pronunciation of the words in the table and underline the stressed syllable in each word.

In many cases, a different syllable is stressed in words in each family, and this has an effect on the pronunciation of the sounds, e.g., 'product: /ˈprɒdʌkt/; pro'duce: /prəˈdjuːs/.

5.2 Find other examples of changes in pronunciation in the words in the table.

5.3 You can also modify the meaning of a word by adding a prefix.

Examples:

interpret   misinterpret

assess   reassess

appear   disappear

5.4 🔊 3.13 Listen to these sentences and write in the missing prefix to each word.

a) All trade unions were declared _____ legal by the government.

b) This is one example of a _____ match between the individual's goals and those of the organisation.

c) They found no significant _____ relation between class size and levels of achievement.

d) Real estate _____ actions rose by 30 per cent last month.

e) Prices are determined through the _____ action of supply and demand.

f) These animals exhibited _____ normal behaviour compared to the control group.

How do the prefixes change the meaning of the original words?

5.5 🔊 3.14 Listen to these sentences and complete them by writing two to four words in each space. Some of the words include prefixes. If you think about the *grammar* and *meaning* of each sentence as you do the exercise, you are more likely to get the correct answers.

a) We had to get _____, because the detail was not very clear on the original ones.

b) Many doctors work _____, which put them under a lot of stress.

c) Crime prevention is _____ of the police's work, but it is often difficult to assess its effectiveness.

d) Doctors have noticed _____, such as bulimia and anorexia, not just among young women but, surprisingly, among young men.

e) These plants should be grown in partial shade, rather than _____.

f) Researchers have found that _____ much more likely to be involved in traffic accidents.

5.6 ◐ **3.15** Listen to these groups of sentences. Complete the sentences by writing two to four words in each space. One of the words in each space is a form of the word in bold.

a) i) Children need a **secure** environment in which to grow up.

ii) Many immigrants are only able to find _____.

iii) The money was invested _____ and property.

b) i) Achievement levels **vary** considerably from school to school in the city.

ii) Some economists believe that interest rates can be predicted by examining

_____.

iii) In the Eden Project they have managed to create _____ of habitats.

iv) There is _____ to health care in different parts of the country.

c) i) How are we going to **solve** this problem?

ii) You need to _____ in water before applying it to the crop.

iii) There appears to be _____ between the two countries, despite years of peace negotiations.

d) i) A mass spectrometer was used to **analyse** the gases.

ii) _____ of the data is needed to confirm these initial findings.

iii) The course is designed to help students to develop _____.

e) i) The results **indicate** that the virus mutates more rapidly than was first believed.

ii) All the _____ suggest that the economy is recovering.

iii) The strike was _____ the level of the workers' frustration.

f) i) Chomsky was a fierce **critic** of Bush Senior's foreign policy.

ii) There was _____ the way the election had been administered.

iii) The negotiations _____ the establishment of peace in the area.

Sound advice: Your listening skills will improve if you work to enlarge your vocabulary. Learning word families is an effective way of doing this, but you also need to develop your awareness of differences in pronunciation between words in each family.

You can learn the most useful word families by referring to the Academic Word List and by doing the exercises in *EAS: Vocabulary*.

Summary of the main points studied in this unit

- Recognising key points and examples in lectures.
- Using your understanding of examples to confirm or infer key points.
- Understanding relationships between ideas in lectures.
- Word stress and pronunciation in word families.

4 Note-taking: Part one

In this unit you will:
- discuss the reasons for taking notes in a lecture;
- learn the principles of effective note-taking;
- practise taking notes from lectures.

Task 1: Reasons for taking notes

Discuss these questions with your partner.

a) Why do students take notes in lectures?

b) What do they do with the notes after lectures?

c) Who are the notes for?

d) When you are taking notes, what kind of information do you need to write down? What do you not need to write down?

Task 2: Principles of note-taking

2.1 You are going to listen to an extract from a lecture on dealing with traffic problems in the UK. Before you listen, discuss these questions.

a) Why do you think there are so many cars on the roads in Britain?

b) What kind of problems does this create?

c) Can you think of any ways of reducing the amount of traffic? What are they?

2.2 4.1 Listen to the recording and read the extract at the same time.

> So Britain's roads, and especially those in the southeast, are overcrowded. There are too many cars on the roads, and at particular times of the day and in particular places, traffic is either very slow or at a standstill. Now this has had a number of effects. Firstly there is the economic effect, all the time wasted in traffic jams, which means a loss of productivity. Then there is the environmental effect. Cars produce a lot of pollution, which damages the local environment, but it also contributes to global warming. And there's also the effect on people's health. In addition to the poor air quality and the damage this causes to people's lungs, the stress of being stuck in traffic each day leads to a higher risk of heart disease.

Now look at these notes taken by a student during the lecture. Then answer the questions that follow.

UK's roads overcrowded → effects
- economic; loss of prod.vity
- environmental; pollution, glob. warming
- health probs.; lung, heart disease

a) Why has the student chosen this information to note down?

b) From your reading of the lecture extract, is there anything else the student should have noted down?

c) Are the notes clear? When the student reads the notes a week later, will she be able to understand them?

d) What techniques did the student use to:

   i) make sure the notes are clear?

   ii) save time?

Look how this student has focused on the key ideas to produce her notes.

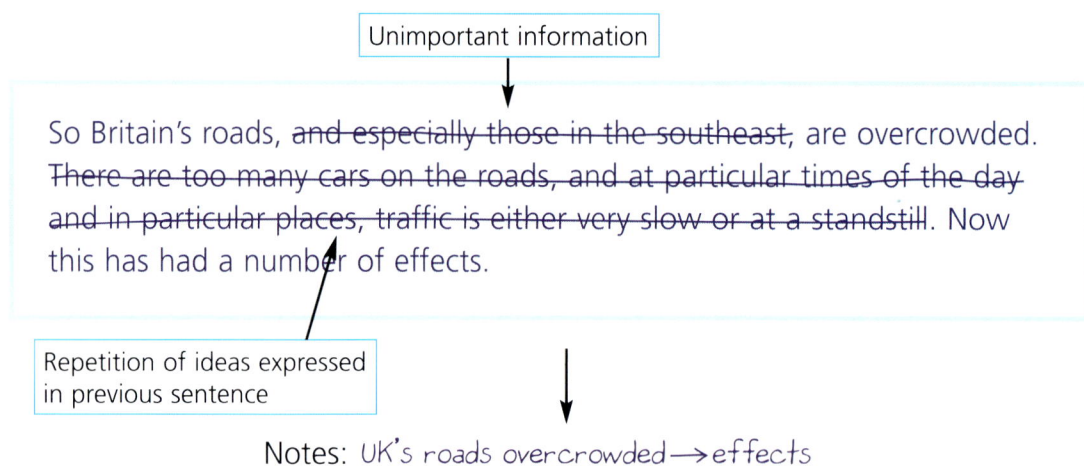

Unimportant information

So Britain's roads, and especially those in the southeast, are overcrowded. There are too many cars on the roads, and at particular times of the day and in particular places, traffic is either very slow or at a standstill. Now this has had a number of effects.

Repetition of ideas expressed in previous sentence

Notes: UK's roads overcrowded → effects

2.3 What do you think the speaker will discuss in the rest of the lecture?

2.4 🔵 4.2 Now listen to three more parts of the lecture and continue the notes here. Before you listen, check you understand the meaning and pronunciation of any key vocabulary given here.

Part two

Vocabulary   policy   measure   integrated

Part three

Vocabulary   consultation   investment

Part four

Vocabulary   (road) lane   CCTV   congestion

Sound advice

When taking notes, you need to be:

- selective: Decide what is important according to the speaker and according to your knowledge of the subject.

- brief: Use abbreviations and symbols.

- clear: Make sure the relationships between ideas are clearly related to each other. When you read the notes some time later, will you understand them?

Task 3: Note-taking practice

3.1   **4.3** Listen to part one of an extract from a lecture on the history of development economics. The lecturer is discussing the reasons for rapid economic growth in East Asia in the 1980s.

a) Before you listen, discuss these questions and check you understand the meaning and pronunciation of any key vocabulary given.

   i) Which countries in East Asia have developed rapidly since the 1980s?

   ii) Can you explain the reasons for this rapid economic growth?

b) Continue the notes, remembering to be selective, brief and clear.

Part one

Vocabulary | liberalism   intervention

Interpreting East Asian economic miracle.
Dispute about influence of market liberalism,
e.g., China ...

3.2 ◗ **4.4** In part two of the extract, the lecturer goes on to discuss another factor.

Part two

Vocabulary | investment   stimulus

Everyone agreed about one element ...

Task 4: Micro-skills: Understanding sentence stress

In the previous unit you saw how *word* stress affects the pronunciation of syllables in the word.
In a similar way, in any spoken *sentence*, certain words are stressed, and this affects the
pronunciation of other words in the sentence.

> And a 'lot of time was 'spent in the nineteen-'nineties trying to in'terpret
> the 'so-called 'East Asian 'miracle.

◗ **4.5** Listen to this short section from the extract in Task 3.1. The main stressed syllables in
this sentence are marked with '.

The speaker chooses to stress words which are particularly important to what he is saying.
These tend to be content words, rather than function words.

One problem in listening is often that the *unstressed words* tend to be:

● pronounced in unexpected ways;

● compressed together, so that it is difficult to hear where one word ends and another begins,
e.g., *a lot of time*: /əlɒdətɑɪm/.

4.1 ◑ **4.6** Listen to another section from the extract in Task 3.1 and complete the sentences by writing one or two words in each space. The stressed syllables in the stressed words are marked with '.

> The Japan'ese _____ 'never run _____ market e'conomy.
> 'Neither _____ the Ko'reans .

a) How easy or difficult was it to hear these words?

b) If it was difficult, could you work out what they were from the context?

4.2 ◑ **4.7** Here is a longer extract from a lecture about market research.

The lecturer is making the point that when you are collecting market research data through a questionnaire, you need to test out the questionnaire on a small number of people to check that it works well before you carry out the real survey. Listen and complete the sentences by writing two to seven words in each space.

> You need to pre-test the questionnaire. This is really important. Those of you, some of you, will be doing this for your dissertation. Some of you, I know, _____ .
>
> You need to pre-test the thing, because you're the researcher. You're very _____ . You know what you're talking about, but you've got to check that other people do as well. And if you want a statistically valid sample of a hundred people or two hundred people, _____ you're collecting the data properly. And it's here that these _____ , they're going to tell you whether it's going to work or not.
>
> So make sure you do pilots, and, you know, this can be, sort of, _____ _____ different people that you question. I mean you'll soon find out whether you've got any potential ... or any doubts about the length of the questionnaire, _____ _____ , or whether the sort of questions that you're asking are valid. You'll soon find out from that. So piloting or pre-testing is really important.

4.3 Now look at the words that you wrote in the spaces.

a) Which words were stressed?

b) Which words were unstressed? How were these words pronounced? Was it difficult to hear them?

Sound advice: Some of the missing words in Task 4.2 are unstressed and difficult to hear. Because they are function words, you do not usually need to understand them to follow the meaning. However, function words often show the relationships between ideas in the sentence, and so it can be important to understand them correctly.

Summary of main points studied in this unit

- The process of making notes and reasons for making them.
- Principles of effective note-taking; being selective, brief and clear.
- Sentence stress and the difficulties of hearing unstressed words.

5 Note-taking: Part two

In this unit you will:
- learn how to use abbreviations and symbols to save time when note-taking;
- discuss the advantages and disadvantages of two ways of taking notes;
- practise note-taking from lectures.

Task 1: Returning to your notes

It is important that your notes are sufficiently clear, so that when you come back to them some time after the lecture you can understand them. Your teacher will show you some notes from a lecture extract that you listened to recently.

With a partner, try to expand the notes into complete sentences, explaining how the ideas are connected to one another.

Task 2: Using abbreviations and symbols

2.1 What abbreviations and symbols were used in the notes which you discussed, and what do they mean?

2.2 Because your notes are generally for yourself, the abbreviations you use will tend to be *personal*. Here are some examples of abbreviations that a student studying economics used. What do you think they stand for?

infl.	**invest.**	**recess.**
bus.	**org.**	**min.**

What abbreviations might you use if you were listening to lectures in your own field?

2.3 What do you think these symbols could be used to refer to?

Symbol	Meaning	Symbol	Meaning
↗	increase, rise, go up	≠	
↘		€	
→		?	
←		!	
≥			

2.4 You are going to hear an extract from a lecture on language learning. The lecturer is referring to a source text (Littlewood) which provides an analysis of the purposes of education in general.

○ **5.1** Listen and continue these notes, using symbols and abbreviations.

Extract 1

3 purposes of education (Littlewood)

2.5 This is another extract from the lecture on development economics. Here, the lecturer is describing changes in the world economy during the 1970s.

○ **5.2** Listen and continue these notes, using symbols and abbreviations. Before you listen, check you understand the meaning and pronunciation of any key vocabulary given.

Extract 2

Vocabulary

inflation	anchored	devalue	float

early 70s econ. boom ⟶ infl. in world econ.

Task 3: Organising your notes

Ways of taking notes

Different people organise their notes in different ways. Some students write *linear notes*, starting at the top of the page and working down, while other students prefer to use *mind maps*. The best solution may be to use different ways of taking notes for different types of lectures.

3.1 Look at these descriptions of different lectures. Do you think it would be better to use mind maps or linear notes for these lectures? Why? Discuss your ideas with another student.

a) This is a lecture on global warming. The lecturer discusses the evidence that global warming is taking place, then looks at the causes, and finally looks at possible solutions and the difficulties of solving the problem.

b) This is a lecture on teleworking. The writer compares teleworking with normal ways of working, i.e., office-based working. He looks at the social, financial and environmental effects/benefits of both types of work.

c) This is a lecture on the history of the European Union from the 1950s to the present day.

d) This is the first lecture in a series of lectures on a course called *Global Problems*. In this lecture, the speaker gives an overview of some of the main problems facing the world today.

3.2 ◖ **5.3** Listen to this extract from a lecture titled *Health in the UK* and make notes. Work with a partner. One of you should take notes in a *linear style*, the other should make a *mind map*.

Before you listen, make sure you know the words in the box. How would you abbreviate these words?

> | individuals | life expectancy | statistics | heart disease | prescriptions |
> |---|---|---|---|---|
> | blood pressure | cholesterol | physical inactivity | British Heart Foundation | |

3.3 Compare your notes with your partner. Which style of note-taking do you think was more appropriate for this lecture? Why?

3.4 With your partner, discuss what you think the advantages and disadvantages of *linear notes* and *mind maps* are. Think about:

● the process of writing the notes in a lecture;

● referring to the notes after the lecture.

3.5 Compare your opinions with another pair.

Task 4: Micro-skills: Word boundaries

4.1 ◖ **5.4** Listen and complete these three sentences.

a) The government has introduced _____ to encourage investment in this region.

b) For _____ these organisations are often regarded as charities.

c) A number of reforms to the _____ have been proposed.

4.2 Did you find it difficult to understand the missing words in the sentences? If so, why?

The pronunciation of a word is affected by the word before or after it. When you are listening, it is sometimes difficult to hear when one word ends and another begins, because it may sound as if the words are linked together. In addition, sometimes sounds are inserted between the words, or sounds disappear or change. These make pronunciation easier for the speaker, but may cause problems for the listener!

🌓 5.5

Linked words: Consonant + vowel

When a word ends in a consonant sound and the next word begins with a vowel sound, the words may seem to be linked, e.g.:

add‿up

What‿are these?

the main‿objective

Inserted sounds: Vowel + vowel

When a word ends with a vowel sound and the next word begins with a vowel sound, a /w/, /j/ or /r/ sound is inserted, e.g.:

do /w/ anything

try /j/ out

no /w/ idea /r/ of it

Disappearing/changing sounds: Consonant + consonant

When a word ends with a /d/ or /t/ sound and the next word begins with a consonant, the /d/ or /t/ sound often disappears, e.g.:

next day

rapid growth

4.3 🌓 5.6 Listen to these phrases and, using the symbols in the examples in Task 4.2, mark them with linking, inserted and disappearing sounds.

a) they invested in property

b) a mixture of oil and residues

c) it's an open market

d) it's due on Friday morning

e) free admission on Sundays

f) it shows as a white mark

4.4 You are going to listen to an extract from a lecture on the theory of real options in investment. Real options are techniques that allow investments to be analysed while taking flexibility and uncertainty into account.

🌓 5.7 Listen and complete the excerpt by writing between two and five words in each space. The missing expressions include examples of word boundaries that may cause you difficulties.

I'm going to go through the theory of real options, and then I'm going to show you how they can be used to _____, particularly on property assets. Real options are a term which was coined ten or 15 years ago, when people began to realise that _____ _____ isn't the only thing you should look at in valuing assets, that a number of assets in companies have _____ _____ option value. And so the option theory that you've been looking at can also be applied to _____ instead of just _____. And that, in raising money, companies particularly have _____ from an option pricing perspective than they first thought. The idea on real options is that management is not just a passive participant, that management can take _____ in making and revising decisions that can lead on from unexpected market developments, such as for example the _____ has gone up from £10 a barrel to _____ £30 a barrel over the last year. So if you were an oil producer this time last year you would be taking a very different view on the _____. So the increase in oil prices has uncovered a stream of options which make oil producers a lot more valuable and now you can bring oil fields _____ that were not necessarily economic. So this is the kind of idea that when we're looking at a project we're just not looking _____, we're actually looking at a cash flow that can be subject to a lot of optionality in it.

Summary of main points studied in this unit

- Reconstructing notes you have made in a lecture.
- Using abbreviations and symbols to save time when note-taking.
- Different formats for note-taking (linear, mind maps), their advantages and disadvantages.
- Linking and word boundaries; how sounds merge, change or disappear at the beginning and end of words.

6 Introducing new terminology

In this unit you will:
- listen to different lecturers introducing new terms or concepts;
- meet different techniques for introducing new concepts;
- practise recognising unstressed function words which may be difficult to hear.

Introduction

Lecturers usually introduce new terminology to their students during lectures. The terms they introduce often represent new and quite abstract concepts which can be difficult to grasp.

Here are some of the things lecturers do to help their students understand new terms or concepts.

- give definitions;
- provide a number of *extended* examples;
- explain how things work;
- contrast the new concept with a concept that is already familiar to the students.

In this unit you will listen to extracts from three lectures and see examples of some of these ways of introducing new concepts.

Task 1: Lecture 1: Embedded words

In the following extract from a lecture on phonetics, the idea of "embedded words" is introduced by the lecturer. She gives an extended example of one embedded word to help explain the idea.

a) 6.1 Listen to the extract and make any notes you want.

Extended example:

b) Check your notes with a partner. How would you define "embedded words"?
c) Think of at least one other example of an embedded word.

Task 2: Lecture 2: EU regulations and directives

In this lecture, the speaker looks at two different types of law within the EU; directives and regulations. Before she explains the differences between the two types of law, she reminds the audience of some of the 'key players' in the EU:

- the European Commission – a kind of civil service;
- the Council of Ministers – a body that consists of the national ministers from each of the member states;
- the European Parliament – which has 626 members elected from all the EU countries.

2.1   Before you listen, check that you understand these words and phrases.

minor technical matters	**regulations come into force**	**opt out**
visas and political asylum	**become legally binding**	**pass a law**

To explain the terms *regulations* and *directives* and the differences between them, the speaker talks about:

- what matters the two types of laws deal with;
- who can issue them;
- when they become legally binding.

2.2   ◗ **6.2** Listen to the extract and complete this table.

	Who issues them	Matters they deal with	When they become legally binding
regulations			
directives			

2.3   Work in pairs. Using your notes from the table, take it in turns to explain fully what the two terms mean.

Task 3: Lecture 3: Market dominance and monopoly

In this lecture, the speaker defines what he means by "dominance". He does this partly by contrasting this new term with a term the students already know, "monopoly".

3.1 Discuss with a partner the meaning of the words:

dominance

monopoly

3.2 Before you listen, check that you understand these words and phrases.

in sole control	**not vulnerable to competition**
a sizeable market share	**the second largest firm**

3.3 ⏺ **6.3** Listen to the extract and make notes on his definitions of both terms.

Monopoly:

_____

_____

Dominance:

_____

_____

3.4 Work with a partner. What examples of monopolies and dominant firms can you think of?

Task 4: Micro-skills: Weak forms of function words

4.1 ⏺ **6.4** Listen to these pairs of sentences. What is the difference in the pronunciation of the **bold** words in each pair? How can you explain this difference?

a) **i)** What time **does** the train leave?

    ii) I'm not sure why he's late. He **does** know about the meeting.

b) **i)** **Some** researchers have taken a different approach.

    ii) We've just got time for **some** questions.

c) **i)** It was heated to 150°C **for** ten minutes.

    ii) There are arguments **for** and against GM crop trials.

d) **i)** I'm not sure what you're getting **at**.

    ii) There were **at** least five errors in the programme.

e) i) Increasingly, small memory devices **can** store large amounts of data.

    ii) Well, I **can** do it, but I don't want to.

f) i) Oh, are they going to interview **us** as well as the students?

    ii) Can you tell **us** what you've found?

4.2 Many *function words*, e.g., conjunctions, articles, prepositions, auxiliary verbs, are difficult to hear when they are *unstressed*.

Look back at the weak and strong forms in Task 4.1. Normally these words are unstressed. Why has the speaker chosen the stressed form in certain sentences?

4.3 In this extract from the lecture about market research, the lecturer is discussing the advantages and disadvantages of using multiple-choice questions.

🟠 **6.5** Listen and complete the extract by writing between three and five words in each space. In each case, at least one of the missing words is a function word.

> Multiple-choice questions – dead easy. They reduce interviewer bias; very easy for people to … very easy and fast for people to answer; very _____. But the argument goes that they are rather difficult to design. The thing about multiple-choice questions is that _____ people into certain answers. This is a good _____. If you have a multiple-choice question and you pilot it, you may find that people are not, they don't put the issue that you're asking them into that particular _____ that you've imposed. So that's where _____ will help. Let me just show you an example of this.

Summary of main points studied in this unit

- How lecturers introduce new concepts.
- The use of stressed and unstressed forms of function words.

7 What lecturers do in lectures

In this unit you will:
- think about how lecturers organise information in their lectures;
- discuss other ways of organising information;
- practise recognising the ways of organising information;
- practise note-taking;
- learn how word stress and pronunciation vary within word families.

Task 1: Introduction: Macro-structure of lectures

Writers use different structures to organise their writing. For example, they might use this structure:

- situation;
- problem;
- solution;
- implications of solution;
- evaluation of solution.

In a similar way, lecturers may also use different structures to organise their lectures. Here are some examples of what lecturers might do during a lecture.

Example structure 1

- suggest alternative methods of doing something
- discuss the benefits and drawbacks of each method

Example structure 2

- state a hypothesis
- outline an experiment to test the hypothesis
- look at the results of the experiment
- draw conclusions from the results

Example structure 3

- present a theory
- see how the theory works in practice
- suggest problems with the theory

Think of lectures you have listened to. Work in groups and discuss these questions.

a) Can you think of any lectures where the lecturers used these structures?

b) Can you think of any other ways in which lecturers organise their lectures?

Task 2: Lecture 1: Doing market research

(See Example structure 1 in Task 1)

In this lecture, the speaker is outlining different methods that market researchers use to get information from people. She also discusses the implications of each method.

2.1   Before you listen, discuss these questions in groups.

a) Have you ever been asked to take part in a market research survey? What did you have to do? What kind of market research was it?

b) What do you think are the main ways of carrying out market research?

c) What are some advantages and disadvantages of each of the methods?

2.2   ◗ 7.1 The lecturer talks about four methods in this lecture. The first is already given here. Listen and write down the other three methods she mentions.

- computer-assisted telephone interviewing
- _____
- _____
- _____

2.3   ◗ 7.1 Listen again and make notes on any implications she mentions for any of the methods.

Task 3: Lecture 2: Social learning

(See Example structure 2 in Task 1)

In this lecture, the speaker is looking at the hypothesis that animals learn from each other, for example, learning which foods to eat or avoid and which animals are their natural predators.

The lecturer discusses various experiments which have been used to test this hypothesis. She describes an experiment where a researcher took a group of 'naïve' monkeys that had been brought up in zoos. The monkeys had never encountered snakes and thus had no fear of them. These naïve monkeys first observed a group of wild monkeys who were afraid of snakes. The researcher then tested the monkeys to see if their behaviour had changed.

3.1   Before you listen, discuss these questions in groups.

a) Do you think animals learn from each other? What do they learn and how?

b) What kind of experiments do you think researchers do to test social learning?

3.2 🔊 **7.2** Listen to part one of the extract on how the experiments were carried out. Complete the notes and label the diagrams.

Hypothesis:

It seems very plausible that monkeys in the wild learn to fear snakes from other monkeys who've already acquired the fear.

Experimental situation:

Observer monkeys

_____

_____

Timetable of experiment:

1 Pre-test

_____

2 Post-test

_____

3 Follow-up test

_____

Procedure of experiments:

Label the two diagrams with these phrases: *neutral stimulus, glass box, food, model snake.* You will need to use some of the phrases more than once.

'Choice circus'

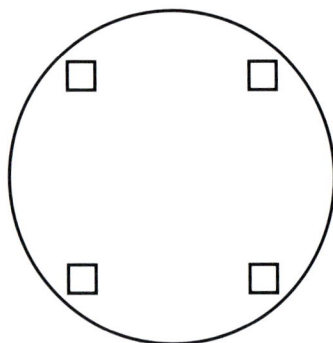

Wisconsin Test Apperatus

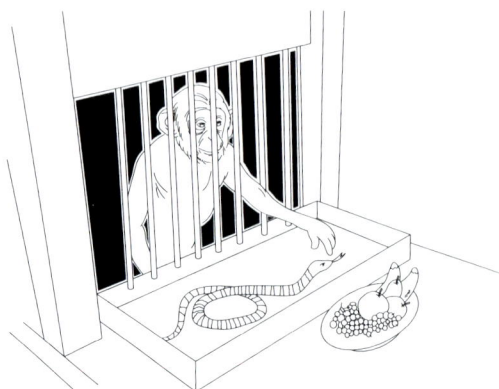

3.3 **7.3** Listen to part two of the extract and make notes on the results and the conclusion the speaker draws from the results.

Note: When giving the results, the speaker refers to a graph.

Results:
The models (the monkeys brought up in the wild):

_____

The observers (the monkeys brought up in zoos):

_____

Conclusion:

_____

_____

Task 4: Lecture 3: Contestable markets

(See Example structure 3 in Task 1)

In this lecture, the speaker is talking about *contestable markets*. He defines them as markets where entry and exit barriers do not exist or are low; in other words, it is easy or cheap for new suppliers to come into the market, and so existing suppliers have to worry about potential competition. The airline industry is commonly given as an example of such a market – especially now that there are many low-cost airlines.

The speaker begins by talking about the *theory* of perfect contestability and what the theory predicts. He then discusses the *problem* with this theory.

4.1 Before you listen, check that you understand the meaning of these words.

> marginal costs   undercut the price   in excess of   oligopolies
>
> inevitable delays   incur sunk costs   monopoly price

Do you think contestable markets are good for the consumers or firms already in the market, or for firms that would like to come into the market?

4.2 **7.4** Listen to the extract and make notes in the space on the next page on what the theory predicts and what the problem with the theory is.

Note: The speaker uses the term *incumbent firm* to refer to companies that are already in the market and the terms *an entry* and *the entrant* to refer to companies that would like to come into the market.

What the theory predicts:

_____

_____

_____

_____

Problem with the theory:

_____

_____

_____

_____

Task 5: Micro-skills: Word families (2)

Many nouns can be formed from verbs by adding a suffix. There may also be small changes in the spelling and pronunciation.

Examples:

Verb	Noun
describe /dɪsˈkraɪb/	description /dɪsˈkrɪpʃn/
prefer /prɪˈfɜː/	preference /ˈprefrəns/
propose /prəˈpəʊz/	proposal /prəˈpəʊzl/

5.1 Change the verbs in the box into nouns and write them in the appropriate column in the table.

> conclude   require   remove   fail   integrate   exist   dismiss
> deduce   consume   acquire   proceed   amend   achieve
> approve   compete   convert   resist   combine

~tion/~sion	~ance/~ence	~ment	~al	~ure

5.2 You will sometimes find when listening that speakers use both verb and noun forms from the same word family in close proximity to one another. Here is an example.

> Although we had **decided** to focus our research on a limited range of fungi, it was a **decision** we were later forced to reassess.

🟢 **7.5** Listen to these short texts and make brief notes in the centre column on the main points. Then listen again for a verb and noun from the same family and write them in the right-hand column.

Topic	Your notes	Verb and noun from same family
a) earthquakes in the UK		
b) hospital workers and radiation		
c) Japan's electronics industry		
d) poverty		
e) behaviour of particles		
f) road safety schemes		
g) male lions in Africa		
h) financial products		

5.3 You will also find that, rather than using a verb and noun from the same family, in some cases you will hear *synonyms*.

7.6 Listen to these short texts and complete them with words or phrases that are synonyms.

a) Many people are _____ that young people lack strong role models, and this _____ has prompted the police to question the conduct of professional footballers, whose actions may have a significant influence on young men.

b) The USA decided to _____ the Moscow Olympics in 1980, in protest at the Soviet Union's invasion of Afghanistan. Four years later, the Soviet Union retaliated with its own _____ of the Los Angeles Olympics.

c) Many multinational companies prefer to _____ local enterprises. Such _____ have a number of advantages.

d) The public's _____ of the government's handling of the economy was critical. While the economy had in fact grown by two per cent, people _____ the high unemployment rate and the government's inability to control strikes as indicators of poor performance.

Summary of main points studied in this unit

- Different ways of organising information in lectures.
- Practice recognising the ways of organising information.
- Practice of note-taking.
- Patterns of word stress and pronunciation within word families.

8 Digressions

In this unit you will:
- look at examples of digressions in lectures;
- examine how lecturers sometimes mark the digressions;
- practise following the lecturer's main points;
- practise note-taking;
- learn a number of expressions commonly used in lectures.

Introduction

In Unit 7 we looked at ways of organising information. However, even where lecturers organise their information well, and explicitly, they often move away from the main topic for a short time before returning to it. These are called *digressions*. There are a number of reasons why lecturers might digress during their lectures.

- to give a short definition of a new technical term;
- to give a reference to a book on the topic;
- to comment on the point they are making;
- to talk about the management of the lecture;
- to give general information about the course;
- to give a personal anecdote to illustrate a point.

When lecturers make digressions, these create problems for listeners. You have to:

- recognise that there is a digression;
- decide whether it is important to make a note or not;
- recognise when the lecturer has returned to the main point.

Task 1: Identifying digressions

1.1 Here is an example of a digression from the lecture on recognising words in speech that you heard in Unit 6. The speaker is talking about the problem of embedded words.

Read the text, including the highlighted digression. Why does the lecturer digress?

> The research that I've been involved in has been looking at factors responsible for our being able to cope successfully with this problem of embedded words. The fact that we're not constantly going off in the wrong direction being fooled by the sounds into hearing something that isn't there. Let's just try to think about what factors might be helping us not to go wrong. I've got three possible hypotheses here and again these are in the handout that I'll be giving you and you don't need to write these down, you'll get this text later on. OK, the question is then, how are we successful most of the time in deciding where word boundaries come?

1.2   This second example is taken from the lecture on social learning that you heard in Unit 7.

🌓 **8.1** Read and listen to the extract. How many digressions does the lecturer make and why does why she make them? How does she mark the beginning and end of digressions?

> My first set of examples come from a – and I'm going to talk about some fairly classic experiments in this lecture, but I would point out before I go on that there is a really excellent chapter on this subject in Shettleworth's book, which is referred to in the reference list for this lecture. Sara Shettleworth has a superb chapter on social learning. It's called 'Learning from others'. It's very up-to-date, very thoughtful, very comprehensive, and I'm just going to mention just a few of the examples that she mentions. But if you seriously want to think about this area, and it involves many complexities, her chapter is a very good place to go. Anyway, some of the best-known work on social learning, or putative social learning, in rats, in animals, are about food preferences. These are examples of learning the significance of stimuli, learning what foods are good to eat and what foods are bad to eat.

Task 2: Practice: First extract

In this lecture, the speaker is talking about how to design questionnaires. In this extract, he is talking about general design issues in preparing questionnaires.

2.1   🌓 **8.2** Listen to the extract and make notes on the main points of his lecture. Do not make notes on his digression.

Compare your notes with another student.

2.2   🌓 **8.2** Listen again and pay attention to the digression.

a)   What kind of information is the lecturer giving?

b)   Would it be necessary to make a note of it?

2.3   🌓 **8.2** Listen again and read the transcript at the back of the book. How does the lecturer mark the beginning and end of the digression?

Task 3: Practice: Second extract

This is a second extract from the same lecture on questionnaire design. In this extract, the lecturer is talking about what people need to do before they carry out market research using questionnaires.

3.1   🌓 **8.3** Listen to the extract and make notes on the main points. Do not make notes on the digressions.

Compare your notes with another student.

3.2   🌓 **8.3** Listen again and read the transcript on page 73. How does the lecturer mark the beginning and end of the digression?

Task 4: Practice: Third extract

This is an extract from a lecture on the history of development economics. In this extract from the lecture, the speaker talks about a development programme known as Integrated Rural Development (IRD).

In this extract, the lecturer:

- gives an explanation of IRD;
- gives an extended example to make his explanation clearer;
- comments on the IRD programme;
- draws a conclusion.

During the lecture the speaker also tells a personal anecdote.

4.1 The lecturer uses these words and phrases in this extract. Before you listen, check that you understand them.

> fertiliser   combat   malaria
>
> an adult literacy campaign   synergy   filing cabinets

4.2 🌓 **8.4** Listen to the extract and make notes on the main points. The four points in the introduction to this task will help you. Do *not* make notes on his digression.

Compare your notes with another student.

Note: The speaker talks about Kenya to illustrate how the programme worked. During the talk, he points to an outline map of Kenya and indicates parts of the country by saying, *'there, there and there'*.

4.3 🌓 **8.4** Listen again and pay attention to the digression.

a) What kind of information is the lecturer giving?

b) Would it be necessary to make a note of it?

4.4 🌓 **8.4** Listen again and read the transcript at the back of the book. How does the lecturer mark the beginning and end of the digression?

Task 5: Micro-skills: Common expressions in lectures

In this activity, you will practise note-taking from short lecture extracts. In addition, you will focus on a number of expressions that commonly occur in lectures.

5.1 The first extract is from a lecture on politics. The lecturer is discussing the issue of whether states are free to act as they please, or whether there are constraints on the way they act.

🔵 **8.5** Listen and complete these notes.

States can't _____ themselves from outside world.
Growth of _____ → states can't _____
what is going on around them _____ has become more
important, and states must respond. Strict appl. of _____
is being eroded.

5.2 🔵 **8.5** Listen again and complete the extract by writing between one and four words in each space.

> I think that realism excludes the possibility – and it's a growing one – that states can simply isolate themselves from the outside world. The growth of television, the growth of mass communications, have meant that it's virtually impossible for states to ignore what is going on around them, and public opinion has become more important _____ within states, forcing states to do things which they might not otherwise do. So the strict application of power _____ maintaining the hierarchy, of ignoring the interests of others, is simply slowly being withered away.

With a partner, discuss what you think the expressions mean.

5.3 The second extract is from a lecture on office design.

🔵 **8.6** Listen and complete these notes.

Scand. ideas impact on Br. office design.
e.g., factors influencing unusual design of offices:
_____

5.4 🔵 **8.6** Listen again and complete the extract by writing between one and four words in each space.

> … ten years later, therefore, we have the Scandinavian ideas impacting on British office design. Another illustration of that might be, you'll discover in _____ the lecture, that some of the factors which are driving the unusual, sometimes, configuration of office buildings on the continent, not always but sometimes, are _____ employment legislation; workers' councils, employers' rights, employees' rights.

With a partner, discuss what you think the expressions mean.

5.5 The third extract is from the lecture on the history of development economics. The lecturer is discussing the impact of the 1982 debt crisis on financial assistance to developing countries.

🌓 **8.7** Listen and complete these notes.

> 1982 – 1992: _____ did not lend money to dev.ing world.
> Only lenders were:
>
> - other governments
>
> - _____
>
> - multilateral agencies, e.g., _____

5.6 🌓 **8.7** Listen again and complete the extract by writing between one and four words in each space.

> Nineteen eighty-two. None of the commercial banks gave any money
> to the developing world for _____ ten years after
> the '82 debt crisis. They got such a bad fright by the debt crisis they
> _____ ceased lending in the developing world.
> So the only people who were lending money to governments in the
> developing world from 1982 onwards were other governments, other aid
> agencies and other multilateral agencies like the IMF and the World Bank.

With a partner, discuss what you think the expressions mean.

Summary of the main points studied in this unit

- Recognising how and why lecturers digress from the main thread of their lecture.
- Picking up the main thread of a lecture after a digression.
- Practice of note-taking.
- Common expressions used by lecturers.

Transcripts

Unit 1

Track 1.1

Task 2.2
Part one

Many students find listening to and understanding spoken English particularly difficult, and I think there are a number of reasons for this.

Firstly, there's the speed at which people talk. Obviously, when people are speaking quickly it's more difficult to understand them.

And then there's the issue of the topic that people are talking about. A topic you don't know much about is more difficult to understand than one you're familiar with. When you're listening to a familiar topic, you only need to concentrate on the new information, whereas if it's a new topic you often have to concentrate on just about everything.

There's also the problem of specialised vocabulary. There may be words you don't know. Now, if there's only a few words like this, people can generally follow the meaning, but if there are key words, or if there are a lot of unfamiliar words, then this can cause problems.

But there are two additional problems you may be faced with if English is not your first language.

When you're reading, you can see when one word ends and another one begins, because there's a space between them. But when you're listening, you can't. You often can't hear when one word ends and another begins, so you have to pick out the words you recognise and, from your understanding of the meaning, the context and your knowledge of English grammar, fill in the gaps.

When students learn English, they're generally reading texts rather than listening to them, so they get used to the written forms of words rather than the spoken forms. But when they learn these words, they build up in their mind an expectation of their pronunciation. And when they actually hear these words in natural speech, they often fail to recognise the words, because they're pronounced in an unexpected way.

So, there are two problems; firstly, it's difficult for students to know when one word ends and another begins, and secondly, they often fail to recognise words which they know in the written form.

Track 1.2

Task 2.3
Part two

So let's look at an example of this. I said earlier that students often fail to recognise words that they hear in natural speech. OK, so let's take the second part of the sentence, "words they hear in natural speech". Now I'd like you to take a pen and a piece of paper and if you could write that bit of the sentence down please. Just "words they hear in natural speech". That part. OK? So you're writing down "words they hear in natural speech". OK, so how many words are there in that phrase? Are there three? Four? Five? In fact there are six. "Words they hear in natural speech." Now when I said this at normal speed, you may have heard "hearinnatural" as one word, rather than three. And you may not have even recognised the word "natural", because you had an expectation that it might be pronounced /natural/ or as /naytural/, instead of /nætʃrəl/, which is how it is pronounced. You might have even heard the word *actual* or *national* instead of *natural*. But the point is, if you saw this phrase written down, you would probably understand the meaning, but when you hear it, it's more difficult for you to understand.

Track 1.3

Task 2.4
Part three

So what is the solution to these two problems? Well, firstly you need to get as much practice listening to natural speech as possible. Listen to extracts from lectures and try to develop your understanding of how words and phrases are really pronounced, not how you expect them to be pronounced. Secondly, you need to accept that when you listen you may misunderstand what is being said. So you need to be ready to change your mind about your understanding of the meaning, if what you hear doesn't make sense compared to what you understood before. And this means taking a flexible, open-minded approach to listening.

Track 1.4

Task 3.2
Part one

Good morning. I'm talking to you this morning because I'm interested in the differences between academic cultures in China and the UK. Now, what I mean by "academic cultures" is simply how students study in the two countries; what are the different components of their courses, what teachers expect from them, and so on. And I'd like to present my ideas to you today and get some feedback from you. The thing I want to focus on particularly is lectures. I'm interested in the difference between lectures, both in terms of how the lectures are organised or presented and also in terms of how the lecture fits into the overall academic programme.

Now, the first question I need to address is, "how do I know anything about lectures in China?" because I haven't studied there and in fact I haven't even been there. Well, I found out by interviewing Chinese students. What I did was conduct a so-called tracking study. That means that you follow students over a period of time. What I did was to follow 12 Chinese students, all doing different courses, different Masters courses at the University of Reading, and over their year of study I interviewed them three times individually. I interviewed them once in the autumn term, once in the spring term and then again in the summer term. And the interviews lasted for about an hour, an hour and a quarter. I asked them a number of questions about studies in the UK and about their studies in China. So my information comes from them and so I have to say right from the beginning that I am talking here about information I got from 12 students, which is obviously a very small sample, and I don't know how representative what they said is of the Chinese education system as a whole. So we have to remember that limitation. I did choose different students from different parts of China, and I made sure that there was an equal number of men and women, and they were all studying different courses here at Reading, so there was a range of backgrounds and experience. But there is that limitation. However, I felt that what I was hearing from the students was actually very similar. I mean, what they were saying individually was more or less the same. So I felt that maybe there is some basis for what they said, and maybe what they did say and maybe their experience was not untypical, in general, of students in China.

Track 1.5

Task 3.4
Part two

OK, so what did I find out? I think the first thing to say it that my impression is that in China the lecture delivers a lot of the content of the course, or the lecturer delivers a lot of the content of the course. And this seems to be especially true at undergraduate level. And just to reinforce this, the students I talked to were postgraduate students. In other words, they'd done undergraduate studies in China. I'm not sure about postgraduate studies in China. But what they said about undergraduate courses was that a lot of the course content came through the lectures. In other words, the students go to the lectures, they make notes in the lectures, and at the end of the term, or at the end of the year, if they have a test or examination, in many cases they simply give back to the lecturer what the lecturer gave to them during the lectures. And that seems to be sufficient to pass the exam and pass the course. So, the lecture is the important vehicle of the course content; it carries the course content.

Now, the second point they made about lectures was that in China they don't seem to be very interactive, in the sense that students sit, they listen, they make lots and lots of notes. But they don't often ask questions during the lecture or at the end of the lecture, and they don't have much discussion, either during or at the end of the lecture, and that is not expected of them. So they really, in China, lectures don't seem to be very interactive.

Another point which students made to me, which I thought was interesting, was that the main points, the important points of a lecture, are often explicitly marked by the lecturer. The lecturer might say, "OK, this point is very important, make a note of this" and might even write things on the blackboard, which the students would copy down verbatim. In other words, they would copy down exactly what he was writing. So this was interesting, it seems that the students don't have to decide for themselves what is important, what is less important. The lecturer tells them. Now obviously that's a very general and very rough caricature of what students told me about Chinese lectures. But how does that compare with the UK situation?

Well, in the UK, I think it's fair to say that the course content is not only delivered through the lectures. If you study on a UK course and if you only give back to the lecturer in examinations, or tests, or assignments or essays, if you only give back what he or she says during the lecture, then I don't think you are going to pass the exam, the course. I think what lecturers are doing in the UK is something different. I think either they are giving an overview of the main ideas connected with the subject, or they are giving some general background to the subject, and then it's the student's responsibility to go away, and to do lots of reading, and to really fill in the details, and to fully understand the theories, the ideas the lecturer is talking about.

And that really brings me to the point of reading. Because what I understood from my Chinese students was that in China, certainly at undergraduate level, they had one course book for each course, and just to emphasise that, they seemed to have one course book. And there was a very close correspondence between what the lecturer was saying and what was in the course book. In other words, if the students wanted to, they could go away at the end of the lecture and read the course book, and it would essentially say what the lecturer himself had said, so there was that kind of reinforcement. In the UK it is very different. There is not one course book for one course. You can't just go away and read one book, and find the entire content of the lectures there. You will have to read a lot of books and a lot of articles to fill in what the lecturer has given you. So in the UK, reading, and reading really widely, is an essential part of what students do after lectures. In China it seems that there is a lot less reading, and the reading is mainly concentrated on this one course book.

That's one thing about UK. The other thing about UK, the UK lecture, is that lecturers here do expect students to interact, to ask questions, to raise points of view, to make comments, to enter into discussion. Now obviously how much discussion there is, how much interaction there is, depends very much on how many students there are in the lecture. Here at Reading, in some cases, we may have 20 students in a lecture and on other courses you may have 200 students in a lecture and obviously there's less discussion if there are more students. There's less time for questions. But interactiveness in general is very important in the UK.

Well, those are just some of my impressions of the differences between lectures in China and the UK, but I would really be very interested now in hearing your opinions. Whether you think what I've talked about is true from your experience or not.

Unit 2

Track 2.1

Task 1.4
Migration

There has been a lot of talk recently in the newspapers and on television about immigration to the UK from countries joining the EU, countries like Poland, and more recently Romania and Bulgaria. This discussion is centred on questions like whether this is good for the British economy or not – in terms of productivity, or impact on national infrastructure, for example on the health and education services, etc. However, that's not the type of migration that I want to look at today. What I want to look at is internal migration, i.e., the movement of people from country to city, and vice versa, and from one city to another.

Track 2.2

Task 3.2
Britain and European Monetary Union

OK, good morning. Well, first up, can you all hear me? Good. Well that's a good place to start. Well, today I'm going to be talking to you about Britain and EMU, the European Monetary Union. As I am sure you know there are now 13 countries in the EMU, or Eurozone as it is popularly known; the last country to join being Slovenia in 2007. You also know, as you are living in the UK and you are using British currency, pounds and pence, on a daily basis, that Britain has not joined the Eurozone. Incidentally, the UK is not alone in this, as other EU countries have also opted out, for example, Denmark. I'll come back to the reasons the UK has not yet joined later in the lecture.

Now I have already talked in previous lectures about the early history of the European Union, or the European Economic Community, as it was originally known, and I also talked about the reasons Britain was reluctant to join the EEC, and why some other members of the EEC, France in particular, were not convinced that Britain should join either. One of the main reasons for this was, I suggested, that Britain felt it had a special arrangement with the United States and with its former colonies in the Commonwealth and didn't want to endanger this relationship by joining. And after Britain's participation in the wars with Iraq, you might conclude that the British still believe they have a special relationship with the US – even if the US may not see this in the same way.

However, leaving all that aside, today I want to talk about three things. Firstly, I am going to talk about the process of how the euro was introduced, and then I'm going to talk about the economic and political tests that a new country has to pass in order to join the euro. However, as the title of my lecture suggests I am going to spend most of the time today talking about why Britain has not adopted the euro, and then about whether I think Britain might join the Eurozone in the future and in what circumstances.

Track 2.3

Task 3.4
Globalisation

Globalisation is a term that you hear everywhere these days, whether people are talking about food – McDonald's and other fast-food companies in particular – or about the economy, with more and more multinational companies all over the world, or about information, with the Internet and the spread of the English language making the same information available at the same time to people all over the world. Arguably, globalisation also includes national cultures, with some authorities suggesting, as I myself do in my latest book, that national cultures as we knew them no longer exist. In any case, globalisation is often said to be the single most profound and wide-ranging change in human history. Ever. Well, that is something you can discuss later, you may have your own opinions on whether this is true or not. But it does go without saying that it is something which affects everybody's life; it affects people as diverse as farmers in the Third World, stockbrokers in London and New York; or global tycoons in multimillion-dollar empire industries. So, obviously, this is something in which a political scientist, or, for that matter, an historian, or sociologist, or geographer, or a whole range of other disciplines, might well be interested.

What I'm going to try to do today is give you some understanding of the history of globalisation, what globalisation means to people on a local level and what its implications could be for the whole world.

So I'm going to be talking on a global scale – which is appropriate for this topic – and I'm also going to be covering some fairly long periods of time.

Track 2.4

Task 3.6
Magistrate's Courts

Good morning, everybody. In spite of what John just said, I'm not going to spend a lot of time talking to you about the family work. That is a specialist area of the Magistrate's Court. As John says, it deals with non-criminal matters involving the state and children. So for example in the case of family break-up it would involve making parental contact orders where the parents can't agree on how much contact time each parent should have with the child, after divorce for example. It also deals with parental responsibility. That means fathers who are refusing to pay for the maintenance of their children. Then finally it deals with any kind of case involving the State and the child. Notably when the state wishes to take the child from the care of the parents and put it in the care of somebody else or in the care of the local authority, the government, and also when the child is to be adopted by another family. But that is another specialist area. What we are mainly concerned with today is the Criminal Court and that is what I am going to spend most of my time talking about this morning.

So this is a court – the Magistrate's Court deal only with offences, criminal offences. So we're not dealing, for example, with disputes between neighbours. For example, if you have an argument with your neighbour about the noise that is being made, or the height of his hedge which is preventing the light getting into your garden – all these kinds of things are dealt with in the Civil Court, but here we are dealing with the Criminal Court so it's crimes against the state as defined by the legal code. So I just want to make that clear from the beginning.

So within that criminal justice system, first of all we are dealing with England and Wales here. There is a slightly different system that operates in Scotland – so we're talking about England and Wales only. Within that justice system there are two main courts. One is the Crown Court which deals with very serious offences. So those would be the ones that you've probably all seen on television where there's a judge and twelve members of a jury. Those are only for serious offences. We are dealing with the lesser offences and those are dealt with in the courts that I'm going to talk to you about today, and that is the Magistrate's Court.

Track 2.5

Task 4.1

However, as the title of my lecture suggests I am going to spend most of the time today talking about why Britain has not adopted the euro, and then about whether I think that Britain might join the Eurozone in the future and in what circumstances.

Track 2.6

Task 4.2

So, for example, in the case of family break-up, it would involve making parental contact orders where the parents can't agree on how much contact time each parent should have with the child.

What we are mainly concerned with today is the Criminal Court and that is what I am going to spend most of my time talking about this morning.

Track 2.7

Task 4.4

Security is an important aspect of using a computer that many people do not pay much attention to. If you buy a laptop or personal computer, you will probably want to connect to the Internet. If so, it is important that you install security software which will protect it from attack by viruses or spyware. There is a wide range of products available on the market which are relatively cheap and which provide a variety of different features. For example, in addition to checking their computer for viruses, parents can use the software to control which websites their children can access. You should not assume, however, that you are 100 per cent safe if you are using such security software. You should make sure that you have backup copies of your work, and you should be very careful about keeping important information, such as bank account details, on your computer.

Track 2.8

Task 4.5

Because of planning restrictions, the large UK supermarket chains are looking to expand their businesses and increase profits by opening smaller "convenience stores". Organisations representing small, independent shops protest that they now face unfair competition from the large chains. And they accuse the large chains of a number of practices that make it difficult for them to compete. Firstly it's alleged that below-cost pricing is used by large supermarkets to force smaller, local shops out of business. Secondly, the large chains often buy up land which is not immediately used, and this prevents smaller local businesses from entering the market.

There is also some concern that the large chains are treating suppliers unfairly. Farmers claim that they are being paid less for their products, and are reluctant to complain for fear of losing key contracts.

However, supermarkets argue that the consumer is the best regulator of the market.

Track 2.9

Task 4.7

Wildlife experts predict that numbers of polar bears will decline by at least 50 per cent over the next 50 years because of global warming. Polar bears rely on sea ice to catch seals for food, and it has emerged that ice floes in the Arctic are disappearing at an alarming rate. Scientists report that the animals are already beginning to suffer the effects of climate change in some parts of Canada, and if there is any further delay in tackling this problem, polar bears may be extinct by the end of the century.

Track 2.10

Task 4.8

Scientists are now able to monitor river levels using information from satellites by using a computer programme devised by researchers at De Montfort University in Leicester. Satellites have been able to measure the height of the sea by timing how long it takes to receive a beam bounced back off waves. But until now interference from objects on the banks of rivers has made it impossible to measure river levels. However, the new programme, which is based on data collected over the last decade, is specially designed to filter out this interference. This new technology will be particularly useful in monitoring river levels in remote areas. It will, for example, enable scientists to examine river level patterns over the entire Amazon river basin, contributing towards our understandings of climate change.

Unit 3

Track 3.1

Task 2.2
Franchising

Part one

Section one (Track 3.2)

The form of business development I'm going to look at now is franchising. The term "franchising" covers a wide range of business arrangements, but today I'm going to focus on "business format franchising".

If you own a small or medium-sized enterprise, you may reach a stage in its development at which, in order to develop further, you need large amounts of capital, or you need to reorganise your business, or to bring into the management team new skills. Let's say you own four or five hairdressing salons in your city which are very profitable. You want to expand the business, but recognise firstly that a lot more money will need to be invested, and secondly that you will not be able to exert the same amount of personal control over the day-to-day running of the business that you have been used to. This stage in the growth of the business may present the entrepreneur with risks that he or she is unwilling to run. However, one way of minimising such risks, while at the same time continuing to develop and profit from a successful brand, is by franchising your business.

Section one (Track 3.3)

So, what is franchising? Well, here is a definition from the British Franchising Association website. And it says, "Business format franchising is the granting of a license by one person (the franchisor) to another (the franchisee), which entitles the franchisee to trade under the trademark/trade name of the franchisor and to make use of an entire package, comprising all the elements necessary to establish a previously untrained person in the business, and to run it with continual assistance on a predetermined basis." This package would include things like training, consultancy arrangements, possibly supplies, marketing on a national scale, etc.

Section one (Track 3.4)

So, for example, if you own a group of successful fast-food restaurants trading under the same name, you may decide to run your business as a franchise. You would allow other businesspeople to open their own branches of the fast-food chain, using your trademark, and in fact you would probably supply a lot of the signage and materials necessary to maintain a uniform brand. In return, the franchisee pays you, the franchisor, an initial fee, that is to say a fee paid at the beginning of the business arrangement, and also an ongoing management service fee. This management service fee is related to the volume of business the franchisee is doing, so it might be calculated as a percentage of turnover, or as a mark-up on supplies provided by the franchisor. So there are two kinds of the fee, the one-off initial fee to set up the franchise, and the ongoing management service fee.

Track 3.5

Task 3.2

Part two

Section one (Track 3.6)

There are a number of issues you need to consider when deciding whether or not to franchise your business. Firstly, there needs to be a relatively stable, long-term market for the product or service you are franchising. This is partially because substantial investment in time and money is required to set up and develop a franchise operation, and partly because you need an established market with potential for long-term growth to attract franchisees. So, something like a chain of hairdressing salons might offer potential for a franchise, because there will always be a demand for women to have their hair cut and styled. On the other hand a franchise to promote and sell a new kind of children's toy might be less successful, because toys tend to have a short market lifespan.

Section two (Track 3.7)

In addition – and this is fairly obvious – you will need a fairly wide margin between cost and income. Remember that the gross margin needs to provide a return on the investment to both the franchisor and the franchisee. So you will need to keep costs low and prices as high as the market will bear. One advantage of a franchise operation is that supplies can be bought in bulk across the whole franchise, which will help to keep costs down. But you can see that franchising would be unsuitable in a market where the margin between cost and income is very narrow.

Section three (Track 3.8)

The franchisor will need to provide support and training to the franchisee because, in addition to the brand, what you are selling is a way of doing business that has proved successful. You will need to produce an operating manual that describes in detail all the different systems and procedures involved in the business, and the performance and quality standards, but you will also have to provide some kind of training for the franchisees and possibly his employees, certainly in setting up the operation and possibly on a regular, ongoing basis. The important point here is that for a franchise to be successful, it should be possible for the franchisee to develop the skills required to operate the business fairly quickly. So, although some initial training may be required, the franchisee should be able to operate the business efficiently and successfully within a few months of start-up. In some types of franchise the skills required may be acquired quickly, in others the franchisee may already have developed most of the necessary skills in previous employment. So, for example, someone operating a franchise in the restaurant industry is likely to have experience either as an employee in a restaurant, or in a similar field.

Track 3.9

Task 4.1

Part three

Section one (Track 3.10)

One further issue you may need to consider is whether the business is transferable to another geographical area. If you have developed your business serving one particular part of the country and you want to set up a franchise network covering a much larger area, the whole country for example, another thing you will have to consider is whether there is a similar market for your product or service in different regions. It may be, for example, that competition in other parts of the country may be so strong that it is difficult for franchisees to survive, or that for localised socioeconomic or cultural reasons the business may not be as profitable.

Section two (Track 3.11)

Finally, when you are setting up a franchise network, you will need to bear in mind that you will be losing direct control of the way your brand is perceived by the customer, so this brings me to my last point, which is to emphasise the importance of protecting your brand. I am sure you are all aware that it often takes a long time to establish a distinctive brand with a valuable reputation, but that this reputation can be damaged comparatively quickly if, for example, quality standards are not consistently applied. The detailed operating manual that I referred to earlier will play a role in maintaining the brand but, just as important, you need to take care selecting franchisees and monitoring their operations. In addition to checking that franchisees have the relevant skills and experience to run a successful business, you also need to ensure that they share the same business values as you, that they accept the importance of maintaining the brand and that they are clear about what they can or can't change about the way the business is run – so people who are very individualistic will probably not make good franchisees.

Section three (Track 3.12)

The written agreement between the franchisor and franchisee should specify very clearly what performance and quality standards are expected, and much of the initial training will be ensuring that staff have the skills to achieve these standards. However, regular visits to franchise units are essential in ensuring that the standards are being applied consistently and uniformly, and ongoing training may be necessary to deal with issues that are uncovered in these visits. Protecting the brand is ultimately in the interests of both the franchisor and the franchisee, because for the franchisee one of the main advantages in running a franchise is that they are buying into and helping to consolidate an established brand.

Track 3.13

Task 5.4

a) All trade unions were declared illegal by the government.

b) This is one example of a mismatch between the individual's goals and those of the organisation.

c) They found no significant correlation between class size and levels of achievement.

d) Real estate transactions rose by 30 per cent last month.

e) Prices are determined through the interaction of supply and demand.

f) These animals exhibited abnormal behaviour compared to the control group.

Track 3.14

Task 5.5

a) We had to get the photos enlarged, because the detail was not very clear on the original ones.

b) Many doctors work long, irregular hours, which put them under a lot of stress.

c) Crime prevention is an important aspect of the police's work, but it is often difficult to assess its effectiveness.

d) Doctors have noticed an increase in eating disorders, such as bulimia and anorexia not just among young women but, surprisingly, among young men.

e) These plants should be grown in partial shade, rather than in direct sunlight.

f) Researchers have found that inexperienced drivers are much more likely to be involved in traffic accidents.

Track 3.15

Task 5.6

a) i) Children need a secure environment in which to grow up.

   ii) Many immigrants are only able to find low-paid, insecure jobs.

   iii) The money was invested in securities and property.

b) i) Achievement levels vary considerably from school to school in the city.

   ii) Some economists believe that interest rates can be predicted by examining key economic variables.

   iii) In the Eden Project they have managed to create a wide variety of habitats.

   iv) There is significant variation in access to health care in different parts of the country.

c) i) How are we going to solve this problem?

   ii) You need to dissolve the pesticide in water before applying it to the crop.

   iii) There appears to be insoluble conflict between the two countries, despite years of peace negotiations.

d) i) A mass spectrometer was used to analyse the gases.

ii) Further analysis of the data is needed to confirm these initial findings.

iii) The course is designed to help students to develop their analytical skills.

e) i) The results indicate that the virus mutates more rapidly than was first believed.

ii) All the main economic indicators suggest that the economy is recovering.

iii) The strike was indicative of the level of the workers' frustration.

f) i) Chomsky was a fierce critic of Bush Senior's foreign policy.

ii) There was some criticism of the way the election had been administered.

iii) The negotiations were critical to establishment of peace in the area.

Unit 4

Track 4.1

Task 2.2
Britain's transport problems

Part one

So, Britain's roads, and especially those in the southeast, are overcrowded. There are too many cars on the roads, and at particular times of the day and at particular places, traffic is either very slow or at a standstill. Now, this has had a number of effects. Firstly there's the economic effect, all the time wasted in traffic jams, which means a loss of productivity. Then there's the environmental effect. Cars produce a lot of pollution, which damages the local environment, but it also contributes to global warming. And there's also the effect on people's health. In addition to the poor air quality and the damage this causes to people's lungs, the stress of being stuck in traffic each day leads to a higher risk of heart disease.

Track 4.2

Task 2.4
Part two

So how do we deal with this problem? It is widely accepted among researchers and policy makers that there isn't just one simple solution. For example, it's generally agreed that simply building more roads is not the solution, as research shows that this just leads to an increase in traffic and, in the long term, it worsens the problems I have just described. So what is needed is a whole range of measures aimed at improving the transport system, which is referred to in the UK as integrated transport policy.

Part three

In 1997 the government carried out a major public consultation on the UK's integrated transport policy. One of the main issues addressed was how we can encourage car drivers to use public transport. The first point is that just making improvements to the public transport system will not be enough to get drivers to use buses or trains. We can provide more buses and trains so that these are less crowded, and we can make them cleaner, safer environments to travel in, and all this will need more investment of course, but even if we do all this, drivers will still prefer to use their cars.

Part four

So, as I said, it is recognised that we need a package of measures to reduce the number of vehicles on the road. Here are some examples.

The government is trying to encourage car-sharing, so, in some experimental projects on crowded roads, lanes have been designated for use only by cars with more than one occupant; CCTV cameras are used to police the trials. The thinking is that if people believe they can get to work more quickly by driving in this faster lane, they are more likely to share cars.

In London, congestion charging has been successful; cars are charged to enter a central zone and again CCTV cameras linked to a computer system are used to ensure compliance. The effect has been that there are fewer cars in what used to be the busiest part of London, but in addition, the income from congestion charging is then invested in London's public transport system.

Well, these are just two examples of fairly small-scale, localised solutions to the problem, but to sum up the point I made earlier, a whole range of measures attacking the problem from different angles is more likely to be successful than one "big idea".

Track 4.3

Task 3.1
The East-Asian economic miracle

Part one

And a lot of time was spent in the nineteen-nineties trying to interpret the so-called "East-Asian miracle". There are big disputes about the extent to which the East-Asian miracle shows that market liberalism works, particularly when you realise that one of these countries is China, with a highly controlled economy indeed. The Japanese have never run a purely free-market economy. Neither have the Koreans. On the other hand, Singapore, Hong Kong were swashbuckling free-market capitalism. So there were debates about the extent to which state intervention in the free market pushed forward the East-Asian miracle.

Track 4.4

Task 3.2
The East-Asian economic miracle

Part two

But nobody disagreed about one element of the East-Asian miracle, and that was investment in people. Country after country in East Asia, it was argued, had undertaken reasonably equitable investments in health care, education and training of people in those countries. And it was argued that this was a major stimulus to industrialisation in this area, that you could always hire a lot of people at low labour rates, but who were in reasonably good health, who were literate and who had reasonable skills. And that was a difference between East Asia and, for example, Africa and Latin America. Or a difference, for that matter, between East Asia and South Asia.

Track 4.5

Task 4

And a lot of time was spent in the nineteen-nineties trying to interpret the so-called "East-Asian miracle".

Track 4.6

Task 4.1

The Japanese have never run a purely free-market economy. Neither have the Koreans.

Task 4.2

You need to pre-test the questionnaire. This is really important. Those of you, some of you, will be doing this for, you know, your dissertation. Some of you, I know, are collecting primary data. You need to pre-test the thing, because you're the researcher. You're very close to the subject. You know what you're talking about. But you've got to check that other people do as well. And if you want a statistically valid sample of a hundred or two hundred people, then you've got to make sure that you're collecting the data properly. And it's here that these pre-tests, or pilots, they're going to tell you whether it's going to work or not.

So make sure that you do pilots and, you know, this can be, sort of, half a dozen different people that you question. I mean you'll soon find out whether you've got any potential … or any doubts about the length of the questionnaire or the style of particular questions, or whether the sort of questions that you're asking are valid. You'll soon find out from that. So, piloting or pre-testing is really important.

Unit 5

Task 2.4
Purposes of education

Three very broad perspectives from Littlewood, on the purposes of education. One is a very traditional one: to pass on value, knowledge and culture. So that you see education as passing from the previous generation down to the next generation, the knowledge they will need. Another purpose of education is to prepare learners as members of society. So you have needs, which you feel your society must fulfil and you view education as a vehicle for doing this. And that will influence how language is taught – we'll see how in a moment. And the third view, which is much more humanistic, a humanistic view of education, is where you see learners as individual selves who must be developed. And the process of education as being developing the self; bringing out the individual's best characteristics, allowing them to learn and to fulfil their potential.

Task 2.5
World economy

What you have to understand is that from the early 1970s onwards there was this primary boom and there were signs of inflation in the world economy. In 1971, America left the gold standard. The value of the dollar had been linked to the value of gold and suddenly the government decided to cut it free. It was effectively devalued. Remember, in 1970 the American economy made up about a third of the total product of the world economy. Today it's about 25 per cent or even less than that, but then the dollar had an even greater influence on the world economy.

So before the 1970s we had fixed exchange rates, but from 1971 America devalued the dollar and the exchange rates floated. And from that moment onwards, the major industrial economies, which in the 50s and 60s had had inflation rates of one per cent, two per cent, three per cent per year, suddenly found themselves with inflation rates running at ten per cent, 15 per cent, 20 per cent. None of you in this room will believe me, probably, when I tell you that in 1971 Britain's inflation rate was 25 per cent, yes. I can hardly believe that as the words come out of my mouth, and I can remember the year very, very distinctly.

Task 3.2
Health in the UK

Well, so much for the problems of health in the developing world.

What I would like to do now is look at the health situation in the developed world, with particular reference to the United Kingdom. I think the situation can be summarised briefly like this: firstly, life expectancy – how long people are living – is increasing. Secondly, we are taking more and more drugs and as a result of this we are curing, or at least controlling, many illnesses. However, what we are not doing as well as we should is stopping people getting sick in the first place.

Let me just illustrate this point with some statistics.

I've said that life expectancy in the UK is increasing and that is true. For example, let's look at men aged between 35 and 74. The number of men in this age group who died dropped by 42 per cent between 1990 and 2000. Now that is a huge fall. Forty-two per cent fewer deaths in this age group over a ten-year period. Now, it is clear to me that much of this fall has been due to the amount of drugs we take now to cure problems.

If we look at heart disease for example, and the drugs we take to regulate or "cure" it, we can see that the number of prescriptions issued by doctors has almost quadrupled – increased by just under 400 per cent – in the last 20 years. This includes drugs to lower blood pressure and to reduce cholesterol. So we are really becoming a nation of pill takers but – and this is the point I want to emphasise – we are not attacking the underlying causes of heart disease. One major cause of heart disease is physical inactivity. And in the UK we are becoming more inactive; we are taking less physical exercise. If you look at the statistics on your handout, you will see these illustrate that since the 1970s the average number of miles travelled on foot has dropped by around a quarter, just about 23 per cent, and the number of miles travelled by bike has dropped by one-third. In other words, we are walking less, we are cycling less. By contrast the number of miles people drive has increased by 70 per cent over the same period of time. So, more use of the car and less physical exercise is the overall picture.

Add to this inactivity an unhealthy diet and the results are disastrous. Look at the figures for obesity in the UK. The percentage of obese adults has almost doubled in the last 12 years; a rise of about 92 per cent. So, as a nation we are becoming more obese as a result of poor diet and a lack of regular physical activity. And what does this mean in terms of life expectancy? Well, over 100,000 people die every year as a result of heart disease. And a third of these deaths – so, more than 33,000 deaths – according to the British Heart Foundation, are premature. In other words, people are dying earlier than they should do.

So, here in the UK we could do more. Other countries are already doing more. Norway, for instance, has witnessed a drop of 54 per cent in the number of deaths in men aged between 35 and 74 in the last ten years of the 20th century. And, as we saw earlier, in that same age group Britain has a figure of 42 per cent. So, although that seems good, we could and we should be doing more, and we should be looking at how to prevent heart disease rather than concentrating only on how to cure it.

Task 4.1

a) The government has introduced tax incentives to encourage investment in this region.

b) For tax purposes these organisations are often regarded as charities.

c) A number of reforms to the tax system have been proposed.

Task 4.2

add up

what are these?

the main objective

do anything

try out

no idea of it

next day

rapid growth

Task 4.3

a) they invested in property

b) a mixture of oil and residues

c) it's an open market

d) it's due on Friday morning

e) free admission on Sundays

f) it shows as a white mark

Task 4.4
Real options

I'm going to go through the theory of real options and then I'm going to show you how they can be used to raise some money, particularly on property assets. Real options are a term which was coined ten or 15 years ago, when people began to realise that net present value isn't the only thing you should look at in valuing assets, that a number of assets in companies have a great deal of option value. And so the option theory that you've been looking at can also be applied to real assets instead of just financial assets. And that, in raising money, companies particularly have a lot more to offer from an option pricing perspective than they first thought. The idea on real options is that management is not just a passive participant, that management can take an active role in making and revising decisions that can lead on from unexpected market developments such as, for example, the price of oil has gone up from £10 a barrel to in excess of £30 a barrel over the last year. So if you were an oil producer this time last year, you would be taking a very different view on the market for oil. So the increase in oil prices has uncovered a stream of options which make oil producers a lot more valuable, and now you can bring oil fields back on stream that were not necessarily economic. So this is the kind of idea that when we're looking at a project, we're just not looking at a static cash flow, we're actually looking at a cash flow that can be subject to a lot of optionality in it.

Unit 6

Track 6.1

Task 1
Embedded words

I've been doing some research on one particular problem that arises out of this and I'd like to use that as a kind of a peg to hang this issue on, to tell you a little bit about it and where we've been getting with this. It's the problem sometimes called the problem of embedded words. So, when we hear a word of several syllables like *responsibility*, a word like *responsibility* invariably contain several smaller English words. So in the case of responsibility we have – you can see here – *response*, *sponsor*, you have *ability* at the end there, and *bill* in the middle there and there's a few others if you looked hard enough you'd find some more. But almost any word in the English language that has more than two syllables will invariably contain within it, packaged up inside it, smaller English words. Now, consider what the brain is faced with if somebody produces a sentence containing the word *responsibility*. If the brain wrongly segments *responsibility* into *response* and *ability*, the decoding of that sentence is going to go catastrophically wrong. You see the point I'm making. So when we hear *responsibility*, it's that word; it's not a combination of "response" and "ability".

Track 6.2

Task 2.2
European Union regulations and directives

OK, so the two types of law I want to talk to you about today are directives and regulations, and these are very different, both in the way they are introduced and also in their scope, in the sense that one of them is more concerned with more serious matters while the other is more concerned with minor technical matters. Anyway I'll return to this in a moment and give you more details and more examples, but before I do that, I want to remind you of some of the key players in the EU, as far as law-making is concerned. You might remember – I hope you remember – that there is the European Commission, the Council of Ministers and the European Parliament, and all these have a role in law-making. The European Commission is a non-elected organisation, which is responsible for the day-to-day running of the EU. You can think of it as a civil service, or the administrators if you like, also called the "bureaucrats of Brussels", which is where the Commission is based. Then you have the Council of Ministers, which consists of one minister from each of the member states, so these are ministers who are part of the government in their own countries. Do you remember this? Yes? No? But that's clear, yeah, it is? Good. And finally we have the European Parliament, which consists of 626 members who are elected in their own countries to work as full-time MEPs, that is Members of the European Parliament.

So, what roles do these organisations play in law-making and what is the difference between regulations and directives?

Well, first, regulations. So, regulations come either directly from the Commission or from the Council of Ministers and they tend to be concerned with pretty minor technical matters, for example, how much beef there needs to be in a beef sausage, for example or, how much real cream there has to be in ice cream. But they are not all trivial or unimportant things. There are regulations about standards of security in EU passports, for example.

And these regulations come into force as soon as they are published in what is called the *Official Journal*. So in other words, on the same day that these regulations are published, people in all the member states have to observe them, unless, and this is very important, unless individual member states have opted out of that particular area covered by the regulation. Let me give you an example of what I mean by opting out. Both the UK and Ireland decided that they wanted to keep control of the whole area of visas and political asylum so they opted out. They said we will not be covered by EU regulation about those issues, so that's fine. So that's regulations. Now what about directives?

Well, there are two main differences. The first is that directives have to be accepted first by the Council of Ministers. The Commission cannot do this on its own and the European Parliament cannot do this on its own. Directives can only come from the Council of Ministers. And even then the directive does not become legally binding in any member state until the parliament of that state introduces domestic laws to give the directive effect. For example, the directive comes from the Council of Europe but it does not automatically become law in Britain, for example. It is only legally binding, it only has legal effect, when the British parliament passes a British law. So it is not the case that we are governed by European laws – many people believe that to be the case but it is simply not true. There have to be British laws. Is that clear? I know it's a bit complex.

Track 6.3

Task 3.3
Market dominance and monopoly

What do I mean by making the distinction between market dominance and monopoly? We all know what a monopoly is, don't we? It's a single-firm case where the firm is in sole control of a market, and it's protected by such high entry barriers that its position is not vulnerable to competition. It's very rare in the real world for such firms to be in that happy position of being a complete monopoly. In the real world, however, you very often find that you have an approximation to dominance. Now, I've got an example … just looking for a single piece of paper. Oh, here we are. I undertook a study in the mid-80s and it was quite easy for me to find 22 markets. The period covered, by the way, was mid-70s to mid-80s. It was quite easy to find a number of markets where the first firm had a share of 50 per cent or above. In some cases much higher; closer to 80 or 90 per cent even. And the second largest firm, or firms, were only half or less of the size, in terms of market share, of the dominant firm. So, although in many cases in the real world, you don't have monopoly – you only find that usually in the case of natural monopoly – the notion of dominance, as I want to use it, is quite frequent. You do frequently find one firm with a very sizeable market share. As a rule of thumb, if you like, upwards of 50 per cent of the market, sometimes even as high as 80 or 90 per cent. And the second-largest firm, or firms, has a share perhaps under ten per cent, or a number of smaller firms all of whom have quite small market shares. Now, I therefore mean by dominance that sort of market structure. The size distribution of firms is highly skewed. You've got one firm in pretty much in command of the market but a number of other firms operating in the market in competition.

Track 6.4

Task 4.1

a) i) What time does the train leave?
   ii) I'm not sure why he's late. He does know about the meeting.

b) i) Some researchers have taken a different approach.
   ii) We've just got time for some questions.

c) i) It was heated to 150°C for ten minutes.
   ii) There are arguments for and against GM crop trials.

d) i) I'm not sure what you're getting at.
   ii) There were at least five errors in the programme.

e) i) Increasingly, small memory devices can store large amounts of data.
   ii) Well, I can do it, but I don't want to.

f) i) Oh, are they going to interview us, as well as the students?
   ii) Can you tell us what you've found?

Task 4.3

Multiple-choice questions – dead easy. They reduce interviewer bias; very easy for people to … very easy and fast for people to answer; very easy for data processing. But the argument goes that they are rather difficult to design. The thing about multiple-choice questions is that you are forcing people into certain answers. This is a good reason for piloting. If you have a multiple-choice question and you pilot it, you may find that people are not, they don't put the issue that you're asking them into that particular set of categories that you've imposed. So that's where your pilots and qualitative research will help. Let me just show you an example of this.

Unit 7

Task 2.2
Doing market research

These are the four sort of most common ways, not necessarily in order, but if you're thinking of how market researchers collect their information those are the ways they do it. Computers are being used to support market researchers a great deal more and the whole business of both selling things over the telephone and doing market research over the telephone has become a very important issue in market research and you'll see reference to terms like CATI; computer-assisted telephone interviewing. I think it probably goes without saying now that when you're phoned up and somebody wants to conduct a market research interview with you, they're probably sitting in front of a PC and we'll look at some of the implications of that. But one of the main ones of course is that the data entry occurs at the same time as the asking of the questions so there's huge savings in terms of that and indeed some of the analysis can go on more or less as you're speaking; things like, you know, in questionnaires you'll need to need to skip from one section to another, well the computer does that automatically. Next week you're going to hear about a technique called adaptive conjoint analysis and this is an analysis method that, as it suggests, sort of adapts to the person who's being interviewed and starts to react or ask different questions depending on the person.

Telephone interviewing is increasing in its coverage, its importance but in some ways it's postal questionnaires that we want to concentrate on today, because it's postal questionnaires that in a sense have to be the most accurate, because postal questionnaires are the ones where the respondent doesn't have any help at all. There may be follow-ups and you may follow up by telephone and so on but it's postal questionnaires which need to be the most accurate, if you like.

Personal interviewing in some ways is very good; very high levels of response, because – although you might have told somebody on the street who is trying to hassle you to answer a few questions to go away – the response rate for personal interviews is actually far higher than these other methods. People find it a lot more difficult to turn away somebody who's sort of standing there in front of them. The problem with personal interviews of course is that the interviewer is there and the interviewer themselves can bias the results and I think it's a lesson in research in general that interviewer bias of course is to be avoided, but if you've got somebody in person and they say "Well how about … ?" or "Do you mean … ?" and this kind of thing and this is where distortions can come in. So, personal interviews are good – high response rates – but there is the problem of bias and of course they're very expensive, you're employing real people to ask these questions.

Telephone interviewing – less expensive but a less good response rate and again some problems of bias. There's a problem whenever you're a person who's asking another person questions. There's always a problem of bias because you want people to expand on their answers and you want people to sort of chat about what they're interested in and therefore you have to interact with them and that interaction is what can cause the biases. The alternative is to have a very strict interviewing schedule and a very strict questionnaire and you do get this particularly on the telephone where, you know, you get this sort of automaton who's actually a person but they're … it's a very stilted kind of interview and some would say that the quality of the data that is collected as a result is not that high. So we're concentrating on postal questionnaires but accepting that you need a good data collection device.

Task 3.2
Social learning: Part one

So it seems very plausible that monkeys in the wild learn to fear snakes from other monkeys who've already acquired the fear. And Mineka set up an experimental situation where observer monkeys could watch – who were of course naïve and didn't fear snakes initially, as you'll see – could watch a demonstrator who previously had learnt fear of snakes, for example, a wild caught monkey. And the question is: What would the observers learn from the demonstrator? To explain the procedure before I show you the data, the observers were tested three times. First of all a pre-test when they were still naïve and they'd never seen a demonstrator acting afraid of snakes; a post-test immediately after they'd seen a demonstrator acting afraid of snakes; and then a follow-up three months later, with no intervening training, to see whether whatever they'd learnt was persistent. And the way the observers were tested was in a choice circus, which was just a round arena with four objects at the four corners, one of which was a model snake, and the other three were neutral objects, and they simply measured how much time the observer monkey would spend near the snake. If they were not frightened of snakes they'd spend about quarter of the time near the snake and a quarter of the time near the other objects. If they were afraid of the snake they'd spend very little time near the snake and much much more time near the other objects. So, how much time they spend near the snake is one measure of fear. The other measure of fear is that they used something called a Wisconsin test apparatus, which is an apparatus simply where monkeys have to reach over a gap to get food and if you put a frightening stimulus in a glass box in the gap, the monkeys will be reluctant to reach over it to get to the food. So in this test they put either a real snake or a toy snake in a glass box and looked to see how slow the observers were to reach over the snake to get a tempting bit of food. And the slower they were and the more disturbed their behaviour, the more frightened they were concluded to be of snakes. So the question is: How did the observers' behaviour change as a function of watching the demonstrators?

Task 3.3
Social learning: Part two

What do the observers do? OK, here they are on the pre-test when they're not afraid of snakes at all, and as you can see they divide their time equally between the four stimuli. They show no avoidance of snakes at all at the pre-test. But at the post-test – when they've had an opportunity to watch an observer who is in the presence of a snake and acting frightened – now they behave not as frightened as the demonstrator monkey, but very much more like the demonstrator. They spend a lot of time near the neutral stimulus and very little time near the snakes. So they have acquired a fear of snakes just by watching another monkey. And this fear is just as strong at the three-month follow-up as it was immediately after. So this is evidence that naïve rhesus monkeys who are not afraid of snakes to start off can learn that snakes are dangerous just by watching another monkey. They don't have to be bitten by a snake or attacked by a snake or anything, they can just learn it by watching another monkey.

Task 4.2
Contestable markets

Essentially, what the theory predicts is that if an incumbent firm in such a market tries to raise its price above marginal cost, an entrant can immediately appear, undercut that price so long as it's in excess of the marginal cost, and still make a profit. So, if the incumbent firm responds and drops its own price to marginal cost, then the new firm, having made a profit previously, can then leave costlessly. The knowledge on the part of the incumbent firm that that is the case – that if it tries to raise its price, or if there are two or three incumbent firms if they try to raise their price, it would immediately provoke entry and the price will then sink to marginal cost – will mean that the incumbent firms will be unable to raise their price above marginal cost. The significance therefore of the notion of perfectly free entry and exit, you can see – well, I hope – it's significant that here was a theory which was saying even if you've got very highly concentrated oligopolies, if these conditions hold, then you needn't worry; there are very few policies you need to adopt towards such industries because they will produce a performance which is in line with that of a perfectly competitive market.

My critique, or the critique of others as well, about the theory of perfect contestability is that if you change the assumptions slightly, the predictions change dramatically. It's very unstable. Let me give you an example of how … of what I mean by that. If in a particular market, for example, which a number of people have said is contestable, if there are inevitable delays between a firm announcing it's coming into the market and actually managing to produce – and if in coming into the market the entrant has to incur some sunk costs – they can only be slight sunk costs. So if there's a delay, a slight delay, between the firm saying I will come into the market, the firm has to build up capacity, there's a delay between the announcement and the actual production, and also if there are some slight exit costs – sunk costs – that the firm has to incur to come into the market, then the predictions of the the model are dramatically different. An incumbent firm in such a market can charge the monopoly price, or if it's two or three firms they can charge near the monopoly price. They can charge near the monopoly price until the entrant appears. They can then immediately drop their price to the marginal cost. The entrant, having finally come in to production, would then make no money, in fact it would make a loss, it would make a loss equal to its sunk costs. If the entrant is aware of that, it would not come into the market. So the sequence is this, that, with slight alterations, if the the notion of a perfectly contestable market is not met, if you make slight changes to the assumptions, even though the market may be approximately contestable, it may make a dramatic difference in the prediction because it means that the incumbent firms will continually be able to charge something approaching a monopoly price. Entry will not occur because the entrants will say, I have to incur slight sunk costs to get into this market, and I won't be able to recover them, and I won't make any money because as soon I appear and produce, the price will collapse to the marginal cost.

Task 5.2

a) Earthquakes are a relatively rare occurrence in the United Kingdom, and when they do occur, they are generally of such low magnitude that they are frequently not recognised as such.

b) Although hospital workers may be exposed to fairly low levels of radiation, measures need to be taken to keep exposure to a minimum.

c) Japan emerged from the postwar period with a developed electronics industry, and its emergence on the global consumer goods market gave European manufacturers strong competition.

d) It is widely assumed that poverty exists only in developing countries, but this assumption has meant the needs of the urban poor in developed countries are often neglected.

e) The particles collide at something near the speed of light and this collision releases massive amounts of energy.

f) A lot of time was spent trying to involve parents in the road safety scheme, because previous experience has shown that the involvement of the local community in such projects is essential to their success.

g) Research has shown that male lions in different parts of Africa behave in different ways when faced with danger. Do environmental factors account for these differences in behaviour?

h) We studied the performance of these financial products over a period of three years, and we found that some perform significantly better than others.

Track 7.6

Task 5.3

a) Many people are worried that young people lack strong role models, and this concern has prompted the police to question the conduct of professional footballers, whose actions may have a significant influence on young men.

b) The USA decided to stay away from the Moscow Olympics in 1980, in protest at the Soviet Union's invasion of Afghanistan. Four years later, the Soviet Union retaliated with its own boycott of the Los Angeles Olympics.

c) Many multinational companies prefer to team up with local enterprises. Such alliances have a number of advantages.

d) The public's perception of the government's handling of the economy was critical. While the economy had in fact grown by two per cent, people viewed the high unemployment rate and the government's inability to control strikes as indicators of poor performance.

Unit 8

Track 8.1

Task 1.2

My first set of examples come from a – and I'm going to talk about some fairly classic experiments in this lecture, but I would point out before I go on that there is a really excellent chapter on this subject in Shettleworth's book, which is referred to in the reference list for this lecture. Sara Shettleworth has a superb chapter on social learning. It's called "Learning from others". It's very up-to-date, very thoughtful, very comprehensive, and I'm just going to mention just a few of the examples that she mentions. But if you seriously want to think about this area, and it involves many complexities, her chapter is a very good place to go. Anyway, some of the best-known work on social learning, or putative social learning, in rats, in animals, are about food preferences. These are examples of learning the significance of stimuli, learning what foods are good to eat and what foods are bad to eat.

Track 8.2

Task 2.1

Now, I'm going to show you lots of examples of different types of questions that you can ask. Here are some very general design issues though. Questions need to be precise, as you'll you'll see in a moment. They need to be well-ordered. Incidentally – sorry, I should have mentioned this earlier – the assessment for this course will, I think, be announced next week, formally, but what it's going to be is a case study. Basically you're going to be asked to evaluate, to comment, appraise. And it'll be a case study describing a, sort of, typical market research process, but it will also include data. There will be data that you can analyse to support your case, and you will be able to analyse it, basically, in whatever way that you want. That'll be up to you. Somebody was asking earlier about will we have to do a questionnaire, and they've probably been talking to people last year who did it where everybody – basically every single individual – ran a questionnaire and it basically just got out of hand. It was extremely difficult to mark because people were producing huge volumes of stuff. But this session now is just basically to introduce you to how this sort of data is collected, but you won't be doing this as part of the assessment. So, your questions they need to be precise, and I'm going to show you some examples of good and bad questions in a moment. You need to decide very carefully, I think, on the ordering. I think there's really not an excuse for it these days, in a sense, for getting this part of it wrong and certainly presentation is very important so we'll talk a little bit about presentation and how you're able to order your questions to make sure that you get – well, there's different schools of thought, but – to make sure that you get an optimum response.

Track 8.3

Tasks 3.1 and 3.2
Second extract: Questionnaire design

So you've got to set very clear objectives as to what your questionnaire is designed to achieve. You need to say something about how you're going to collect the data, the sorts of question that you're going to have, the way you word them, the flow of the questionnaire and so on. Obtaining approval is very important. In the university we have a body known as the Ethics Committee. Technically speaking, if you go out, well if you go outside the university to research anything, you need to get the approval of the Ethics Committee. And the Ethics Committee is, in many ways, a very good idea. The university, and indeed any market research body, that doesn't want its name pulled down by the market research process, of course, and so we have to, if we're going out and indeed if students are doing projects, we have to get the implicit approval of the Ethics Committee. Sometimes that can come from the head of department.

But two or three years ago, just for your information, this group was actually a group of undergraduate students, decided to do a market research project which was part of the assessment for the course. And they were given a free choice as to what subject they wanted to ask people about. And the explicit instruction was that the people they researched should only be members of the course. And this group came and said we want to do a kind of a sex survey. And what this was, it was actually fairly innocent, although I did say, you know, this must be kept strictly within the group, and it, sort of, well, I won't go into the details, but it was asking various pretty personal questions really. And the next thing I heard, the next thing I heard of it, was somebody called up from – I can't remember where – but they'd actually been accosted by one of these students somewhere downtown and been asked these questions. And as you can imagine we got into a little bit of trouble about it, and we hadn't cleared it, I hadn't cleared it basically with the committee, because it wasn't, I didn't believe it was going out – I didn't think it was going outside. So, anyway, there are, obviously very potential problems in that, but you do need to obtain approval. There is a market research society code of practice on asking questions, on how to do research.

You need to pre-test the questionnaire. This is really important. Those of you, some of you, will be doing this for, you know, your dissertation. Some of you, I know, are collecting primary data. You need to pre-test the thing, because you're the researcher. You're very close to the subject. You know what you're talking about. But you've got to check that other people do as well. And if you want a statistically valid sample of a hundred or two hundred people, then you've got to make sure that you're collecting the data properly. And it's here that these pre-tests, or pilots, they're going to tell you whether it's going to work or not.

So make sure that you do pilots and, you know, this can be, sort of, half a dozen different people that you question. I mean you'll soon find out whether you've got any potential … or any doubts about the length of the questionnaire or the style of particular questions, or whether the sort of questions that you're asking are valid. You'll soon find out from that. So, piloting or pre-testing is really important.

Tasks 4.2 - 4.4

Third extract: Integrated rural development

Now here's an idea out of the seventies, IRD, integrated rural development. This was the idea that when you worked in rural areas with the poor, and the smallholder and so on, what you tried to do was deliver a package of assistance across sectors, on the grounds this would give you synergy.

Now just to give you a fairly exaggerated example, if you're trying to get people to plant new varieties of rice and use fertiliser to increase their yields, which you hope is a scale neutral technology that can be used by smallholders, then why not at the same time combat malaria, inoculate people against disease, clean up the water supply? Because all of those will give you better health, which is a good thing in itself but, of course, healthier farmers can work harder in the fields and so that complements the agricultural measures. And while we're at it, we're going to build some access roads, because that will improve price relatives at the farm gate and reduce isolation. And while we're at it, we'll run an adult literacy campaign, because literate farmers can read the labels on fertiliser packs, and so on and so forth.

So there was the idea that you should try and do things in development in an integrated fashion across all sectors, because you get synergy, and you get more than the sum of the parts going on. Now integrated rural development was very, very exciting to work in. You got all kinds of things to have a go at, and you've got quite a lot of resources to play with, but these resources were limited compared with needs. So what happened with integrated rural development was within any country, what you did is you took a country, and a country might look just like that, and it might have its capital there, and you take a country that looks just like that, and you do integrated rural development and you do it there, there, there, there, there, oh and there. And yes, that is to scale yes, that is to scale. In other words, you get these little enclaves of very small areas, where donors are putting in resources and everything is done.

And in the early 1970s Kenya had six small integrated rural development programmes, which were very well documented and some contemporary, very influential thinkers about development worked on those projects in the early 1970s. But look how tiny they are. That really is to scale. These things were in very small areas indeed. Why? Because, although you could target resources for a small area, you couldn't have the whole country running the kind of programmes that were run there. So because you did everything in integrated rural development, you could only do it on a small scale, concentrated in particular areas.

Now those six small experiences, I think, were all successes. They were successes, but I think, with the benefit of hindsight, we would have to say they were unrepeatable and institutionally unsustainable. When the donors got bored, and the funds ran out, and the foreign experts' contracts ended, and the Land Rovers began to rust, these projects essentially stopped. Indeed, I arrived in this part of Kenya in 1979, which had been the administrative headquarters, and there were two or three filing cabinets chock-a with files in my room. And I left them there for a while, and then one day I thought, what on Earth? And I went through these filing cabinets, and it was sort of all the stuff on, sort of, four or five years, ten years earlier, of the implementation of this. Minutes, plans, documents, contracts, budgets, semi-annual reports, monthly reports, all this kind of stuff. And I looked at this, and I said, my goodness, this is a vital bit of development history here, but it's clogging up my office. So it all went in the skip. There's never, never enough historians around to document these experiences, and that's the sort of way. And as I threw them into the skip, I thought, there you go, good idea at the time, good people working on it, quite a success, but not sustainable.

Track 8.5

Tasks 5.1 and 5.2

I think that realism excludes the possibility – and it's a growing one – that states can simply isolate themselves from the outside world. The growth of television, the growth of mass communications, have meant that it's virtually impossible for states to ignore what is going on around them, and public opinion has become more important in some respects within states, forcing states to do things that they might not otherwise do. So the strict application of power in terms of maintaining the hierarchy, of ignoring the interests of others, is simply slowly being withered away.

Track 8.6

Tasks 5.3 and 5.4

… ten years later, therefore, we have the Scandinavian ideas impacting on British office design. Another illustration of that might be, you'll discover in the course of the lecture, that some of the factors which are driving the unusual, sometimes, configuration of office buildings on the continent, not always but sometimes, are to do with employment legislation; workers' councils, employers' rights, employees' rights.

Track 8.7

Tasks 5.5 and 5.6

Nineteen eighty-two. None of the commercial banks gave any money to the developing world for the best part of ten years after the '82 debt crisis. They got such a bad fright by the debt crisis they more or less ceased lending to the developing world. So the only people who were lending money to governments in the developing world from 1982 onwards were other governments, other aid agencies and other multilateral agencies like the IMF and the World Bank.